For Nina,

With thanks
and love,

Jane,

APRIL 2000

Poets Around London And Home Counties
2000

poetry *Pt* today

POETS AROUND LONDON AND HOME COUNTIES 2000

Edited by Rebecca Mee

First published in Great Britain in 2000 by
Poetry Today, an imprint of
Penhaligon Page Ltd, Remus House, Coltsfoot Drive,
Woodston, Peterborough. PE2 9JX

A Catalogue record for this book is available from the
British Library

ISBN 1 8622653 4 8

Typesetting and layout, Penhaligon Page Ltd, England.
Printed and bound by Forward Press Ltd, England

Foreword

Poets Around London And Home Counties 2000 is a compilation of poetry, featuring some of our finest poets. This book gives an insight into the essence of modern living and deals with the reality of life today. We think we have created an anthology with a universal appeal.

There are many technical aspects to the writing of poetry and *Poets Around London And Home Counties 2000* contains free verse and examples of more structured work from a wealth of talented poets.

Poetry is a coat of many colours. Today's poets write in a limitless array of styles: traditional rhyming poetry is as alive and kicking today as modern free verse. Language ranges from easily accessible to intricate and elusive.

Poems have a lot to offer in our fast-paced 'instant' world. Reading poems gives us an opportunity to sit back and explore ourselves and the world around us.

Contents

Losing Her Marbles

She looks the same,
Seems the same -
More bent perhaps -
But still that simple girl,
Eager to please as ever was.

Somehow her thoughts
Have lost their moorings
And drifted down those flowing rivers
Which join oblivious seas,
Swirling round continents,
Innocently adrift.

What can I say
That will retain an echo
In the muddle of her mind?
What can I do to anchor her
In some kind harbour
Where she may be herself again
And know the day?

Acrid old age
Has kidnapped her
Long before death's dispatch.

Sylvia Dewhirst

We Were There

There was no mystery in the life giving goddess, in being totally
eclipsed.

But the light it created, the different colours, as in night, it scares the
unknown animal.

It took the sickly tinges, and raked the stomach lining.

Shadows dwelled in long robes, and silence became general.

Corpse fingers traced decadent, across bored minds.

The degrees dropped, the cool came as death, swift and unhindered.

Then she was gone, black smooth perfectly sphere, then, the dazzling
Zirconia or a rarely glimpsed star.

White gold abundant. It broke loose of the suffocating circle and
began to brazen itself, bring sense to the world once more.

A phoenix of infinite wonder, and the reaper fled.

Stuck to the earth, but effluent our souls, unreason, untamed,
emotion.

Everyone's spirit bonded, a moment of unity, alike, same, small,
unimportant.

Now, with the last wane, the amnesia begins.

A soft memory of excitement and uniform lingers.

Lost the drama, the oasis, the death definers.

How great we thought as witness, still, it was merely a natural dance.

It was a play for the majestic, which is now the down treated and
trodden.

But we were survivors, the awe-struck, the together, we were the
great eyes of our time.

We saw our queen of elastic fluid, struck dumb by a mere rock.

And as in turn, our faith became questionable.

We arrived, we watch, we understood, we forgot, we were and
became cynical, we were unenlightened.

We are the satellite, unknowing of the gravity, of which we were in.

We became I, and I became blind, and blind became normal.

And still in its sky the sun shone.

J Cross

On The Exe

Sleep to soft lulling of waves
High on a cliff in Devon
Early morning cry of gulls
Swish of fishing trawler.

Sunrise over sandy bay
Rabbits scurry by
On clifftop
Blaze of wild flowers
Twitter of birds
Speedboats race
Swimmers dive
Walkers stroll on clifftop.

A world apart -
A place of peace
And infinite tranquillity.

Jenny Hamilton

Yorkshire Dales

Long before my forebears had trod this way
Who laboured in the lee of sodden dales
Under sheer limestone ridges, cutting scales
Of slate to build dry walls, furious, grey,
Uncompromising skies through night and day
Beat savage rain unceasingly in gales,
Scalloping mountains, as in ancient tales
Of gods, who carved stone monuments from clay.

Breaking, the strained voice of a curlew cries
And then is heard no more. I walk alone
Where the wind unravels what thoughts it can:
The years, the years, weeping on older skies,
Run relentlessly like a current down
Still closer to the place it all began.

D W Fincham

The Way, The Truth And The Life

I am the way, the way to go forward,
I am the truth, that will set you free,
I am the life, in me, you'll find comfort,
I am your Lord, please listen to me.

I am the way, to lighten your spirit,
I am the truth, that will break your chains,
I am the life, I died to save you,
I am your Lord, who eases your pains.

I am the way, my spirit will guide you,
I am the truth, where lies turn to dust,
I am the life your father who loves you,
I am your Lord, in me shall you trust.

I am the way, the way everlasting,
I am the truth, the light of the world,
I am the life, to lead you from darkness
I am the Lord, over all the earth.

Alison Shepherd

Killing The Lifeboat

We are stealers,
who take and never give.
We fight our selves,
under the sails, under the shadows,
under the trees, way up on the hills.
The shadows are turning,
tuned to time and light,
as the answers swim in the seas.
We are thieves, busy stealing,
clever hoarders, deaf to the music,
blind to the water,
flowing over our feet,
over our heads.

J Walker

News At Ten

A falling chimney crushed a man in rubble
While I was playing golf
In Ireland bombs and murderous trouble
While I was playing golf
By the M1 a woman lay dead
While I was playing golf
Someone had battered in her head
While I was playing golf
A child fell from an express train
While I was playing golf
Refugees crouched in mud and rain
And I was playing golf.

Georgiana Melrose

The Tunnel

In heaven there is no time,
No waiting around.
All we have ever cared for
In self-forgetfulness,
Ever found wonderful,
Ever felt grateful to,
All that with joy surprised,
Forms in which God went disguised,
Waits at the other end
Of the tunnel of being, of love,
Of birth, of the circus tent.

In heaven there is no time
For truth does not change
Though the seasons revolve,
Though all is recycled, fades,
Falls into blackness, springs,
Spurts into green again.
Truth is what all things are,
The heart of the light itself,
The dance of the particles
That says, 'I am glad to be.'

Sun's light upon the sea
Fragments into flashes.
God's unbearable brightness
Breaks into myriad faces,
Star-shining, welcoming,
Healing, unending embraces,
The longed-for release,
Oceans, skyfuls of blessing,
Great waves of peace.

Margaret Lewis

Stranded In Russia
(Dedicated to Lilia Dashives)

Lilia my love,
    You are free my skylark,
With your wings and plumage
    So beautiful to see.
Only could an imaginary mind create,
    The brilliance of paradise within you.

This human quest that rushes upon us,
    Has sought us and painted us a colourful journey.

What can you feel upon closing your eyes?
    May the possession take you beyond, or
May you find yourself beside a brook of bubbling water,
    So fresh and clear, with a transparency
The might find us an oracle beneath.

Could there be more, where the life,
    It flourishes, with golden nuggets bedded down,
Talking with glint and chatter
    In sunlight and shade,
And affectionately musing in the eternal ever-glade.

My love would take thee to my bed,
    And would lay us together until dawn;
For my heart it is within thee
    With fondness and love,
And to you, truly a kiss so gentle.
    I am yours with friendship for always.

Anthony Rosato

Wishing

How I wish I was there,
  Like the bird up in the air,
Flying there without a care,

How I wish I was there,
Flying there without a care,

Where he goes no one knows
  Maybe where wind blows,
How I wish I knew where he goes,
Flying there without a care,
I would love to join him there
Flying without a care.

  Winter flowers

Where paths are frosty, woods are wet
  I haven't seen a snowdrop yet
But am enjoying the sensation
  Of living in anticipation,

One day when the snow is shrinking
  and I am glancing down unthinking.
There will be snowdrops, white and sweet,
  Encased in green about my feet,

And if by chance the time is right
  To find a winter aconite
Then will I say with words
  Sincere
'O what a happy time of year.'

  Rose L Vincent

Koh Samui

One beautiful island,
many beautiful souls.

Palms stretch over handfuls
of people from all walks of life.
Beach bars clutter the beach skirts
while merchants roam. Blazing heat
touches the raw land, while tropical birds
tweet their tantalising tunes. Thatched bungalows
make up the vicinity, breathtaking waterfalls, wrapping paper-
coloured buddhas, coconut trees, flamboyant flowers, caramelised
sand, transparent waters and complete serenity make the island
what it is.

Natasha C Piris

Silent Pain

No one knows what we go through
    All the pain
All the hurt
    All the suffering
Why don't they help us?
    Why are they afraid?
Afraid of what they'll discover?
    It surrounds us all
Why can't we escape from it?
    It haunts us
We try to run
    But we can never hide
Why do we feel pain?
    Why do we hurt?
Why do we suffer?
    We are pushed aside to a corner
An outsider to society
    Do you think we enjoy being like this?
Don't you think we want help?
    But who is there to help us?
No one
    We are all alone
In our own dark world
    Suffering
Crying out for help
    But no one can hear our cries of despair
One day someone may listen

    But will it be too late?

    Kathrine Cattermole

The Stethoscope
(To Joanna on starting her training as a Doctor)

In my simplicity
I have held the ring
More than a century -
Since Laënnec stretched his ear
To the heart's diploid swing.
The shouts and whispers of the bronchial tree
First came over clear
Through me,
When from the Babel
Of the chest
I could at will
Extract, select, interpret, label
Silence or sound - the rest
Reject as overspill.

Mapping the contours of the heart
I hold privacy
Against bureaucracy;
Saving its trusted data
From the computer's hoard -
Or, later
The ex-cathédras of the all-wise Board.

Amplifying
Without electronics
The gut's harmonics -
I am a gut-reaction too,
Dressed for the part
To cry defiance
On all complexities of modern science.
- And long live elemental Hippocratic Art!

Edward Smyth

For Eddie

Beside a Yorkshire lake
or Scottish glen
whatever route you take
I'll be there, you ken?

I'll be in the gentle breeze
and from the sky I'll fall
to earth amidst the majestic trees.
I am the cool droplets of rain
listen for me, I'm trickling down your windowpane.

The crunching Autumn leaves underfoot,
the faraway sparkling stars that twinkle
on nights as dark as soot.
I am all of these and more
I am the bricks in the local store.

I have ten thousand eyes
and one hundred thousand ears,
I hear all your sighs
I see all your tears.

One day, together again we'll be
partners for all eternity.

Ian Mowatt

Bullet

Silvered, steeled, polished round
Racing, silent screaming above the ground
One direction, just one mission
Bound on target, maintain position
Slicing, carving, clean through air
Brace for impact, eyes fixed and stare
Target found, straight, true, penetrate
New feelings, wounds, communal fate
Unholy two together now lie
As in each other's arms we now die

A C Dancer

Trams Full Circle

Once I stood, as a child, at 'The Broadway',
Felt a thrill to hear trams rattling by;
Perched on rails (for grooved wheels), not designed for high heels,
And with long metal arms to the sky.

How we clung to our seats round the corners,
As they lurched with a rock 'n' a roll;
When the arms lost their grip, from their cables they'd slip,
But a man put them back with a pole!

All so highly efficient in those days,
In their quaintness, a joy to behold;
Sadly, those joys are gone, as the world stumbles on,
Leaving me far behind, growing old.

> Technology : manicology!
> Mobile 'phones,
> so attractive, radioactive?
> TV ads. corn;
> www.porn.
> GM veg., contam.meat,
> food nobody wants to eat.
> Overloads; congested roads.
> Forget Aristotle -
> grow a clone in a bottle.

> Where are we heading?
> Turn again Whittington!

Now I stand one more time at 'The Broadway',
And the sight brings a tear to my eye;
Half a century gone; my God, how we've moved on,
There's a new, shiny tram gliding by!!

Mary Halfpenny

The Call Of The Hills

It rained today
    and the cold, mist covered hills called to me.

It rained today
    and yet I longed to be above the grey old town where tourists
        damp and umbrella'd,
            hustled into cafes and shops.

        I feel the hills call to me, silently, as if a silken thread is
                            attached to my heart.
        It tugs but it does not hurt, such a gentle pain it is.
        Yet it instils such urgency I can scarce stop from setting off at
                            once.

        They call, 'Come, see the tumbling waterfall, and the bubbling,
                        gurgling becks.
        Come, feel the granite 'neath your boots; the pull of working
        muscles in calf and thigh. Feel the pleasure when you scan the
                    view from way on high.'

It rained today and I ignored the draw of high places
    watching the swirling mists upon the Fell (between ironing
        and cooking), yet feeling the lure of the hills.

It rained today; cold, driving, icy rain. Not a day to be out.
    I sat by pine log fire and read.
Then quietly, reluctantly that night I went to bed,
    with just one thought in mind;

    Tomorrow, I will climb those hills,
    Come wind or hail and rain,
    Tomorrow, I will climb those hills,
    To ease that gentle pain.

    J Stubington

Abandoned

The thoughts of roots,
    Invade my dreams
Ancestral longings
    Intrude the schemes
No memories stir, nor credence yields
    No genes, or heralds, to engrave and on shields
Unwanted, unplanned, a life reflected
    A severed cord, a life rejected.

Teenage years, the unyielding tears
    Stifled thoughts, unwanted fears
A carbon of life, that never was shown
    Compassion, forgiveness, actions not known
Deep down is sorrow and longings persist
    Anger not hate continually exist
But the love of a mother, forever is strong
    Will live in your heart, and never be wrong.

E Croker

Vermilion Days

He wrapped himself around me like a Chinese festival dragon,
His red shirt was the remnant of an arrogant matador's cloak.
As serpents do he writhed and coiled about me,
As his whiskers whispered daringly at my throat.
A spectre that sparkled like an old-time dance hall sphere,
With feet nimble almost naughty in soft Italian lace-up shoes.
My arching back became a path across the bridge of time,
Upside down dreams, Latin lovers and stiletto heels.
Work worn hands held me as I twirled and clasped,
His cheap giant gemstone rings grinding in my palm.
Smell of musky after-shave reminded me of visitors to Cuban

brothels,

Pool blue eyes watered, as in the smoky atmosphere of a seedy night.
Six pearly shirt buttons dazzled me like a slow daylight eclipse,
Drawing down the slim body and slightly sensual hips.
His flat belly enabled us to clone two bodies urgently together,
As required at climax then diminuendo of the Latin rhythm.
Chest hair curling from beneath that blood red robe,
So stark against my own blonde bee-hive hair.
Later would I recall the soft voice spoilt by a put-on accent,
As his breath lingered on my now flushed and powdered cheek.
My black chiffon swished to and fro as I trod the wooden boards,
Paste diamante necklace thumping on my heaving chest.
Calf muscles straining to the powerful beat of the band,
Gripping his indented back so there is no escape. Locked together
By the sweaty closeness of two beings acting out a dream,
The red lipstick flame of passion passed between our pouting lips.
Something to fill up endless hours of winter solstice afternoons,
In the carnival of living, could it be a tango had become my way of

life?

Jennifer H Fox

What Draws Me To The Woods This Wintry Day?

What draws me to the woods this wintry day
When fog is freezing and the drifted snow
Lies deep in comely hummocks all the way
Along the hedgerows where I go?

So cold a magpie on a garden prop,
Not warily all eyes and wit,
But tamed and humbled by its empty crop,
Waits, like a robin or a tit.

I go to stand in silence by a tree.
So close and still against the bole,
The lichen and the bark grow part of me,
And simply being awes my soul.

Then does the skimming hawk swerve by my eyes;
The stealthy pheasant scratch my feet;
The trotting dog-fox pause in mild surprise,
His unexpected guest to greet.

Then when the restless deer, all nerves and ears,
Browse doubtfully around my tree,
Within my brain an ancient instinct stirs
And makes me part of what I see.

Bob Davies

Knit 2 Purl 2
(For Simon and Sandie)

Grandma Biggins couldn't rest
Started by knitting her winter vests
Then her knickers edged with blue,
Said it gave her something to do.
Then followed pleated skirts and blouses,
Men's underpants and shirts and trousers
Gloves and scarves and coloured hats
Cushion covers and table mats.
Rugs and blankets, single and double,
Said it wasn't any trouble!!
Then a curtain for the door,
And even a carpet for the floor.
School uniform in grey and red.
And blue striped pyjamas, for bed.
Knit and Purl, Aran and cable,
Knitting piled up on the table.
Young Simon said, 'I feel a fool
Wearing all this stuff to school.'
Said, 'I'd like a tracksuit all in blue,'
And Mother said, 'I'd like one too.'
Sandie dancing round the kitchen,
Said, 'I'd like a dress with fancy stitching.'
Down to the shops they all paraded

While they were gone, giant moths invaded
Clothes and blankets, they attacked
Through everything they munched and hacked.
When they came back and opened the door,
Only the furniture stood on the floor!!!

V M Catlin

Night Predator

Sleep by day and hunt by night,
Never-ending tireless flight.
On silent wings the owls glide,
Gives no chance to run and hide.
A predator that's never seen,
But with eyesight oh so keen.
Long Eared and Short, Barn and Snowy,
All with plumage oh so showy.
Ghostly spectres one and all,
When from out the sky they fall.
Unsuspecting on their prey,
Who'll never see the light of day.
Solemn, wise, nocturnal bird,
Seldom seen or seldom heard.
Awaiting for dawn's early light,
Sleeps by day and hunts by night.

Alun Harries

Tintern Abbey October 1999
(with apologies to Wordsworth)

Nearly a thousand years ago
Cistercian monks built on these hills
with love, to praise their God (our God?),
the first foundation of this mighty Abbey;
the arches open now up to the sky,
soaring above the trees
which sing a silent hymn of green and gold;
Once, psalms did soar
up to those arches built of mellow stone.

The sky is bright as hope,
bedecked with wings of cloud.
Beauty and faith and hope
baptise our spirits here,
two thousand years since the Jew, Jesus,
taught a way to peace.
Despite 'holy wars' and ethnic slaughter,
many there are who walk the way in love,
knowing that all are One in the Eternal seed.

Jean de Leon Mason

If I Could

If I could climb a mountain,
And stand above the world I knew.
I would walk to the very top,
And shout that I love you.

If I could tell the world,
Of what a wonderful person you are.
Then everybody would soon know,
That you are my brightest star.

If I could take my heart out,
And show all my care.
You would soon realise,
That you are always there.

If I could give you the world,
With all that's in it too.
It wouldn't total to as much,
To the amount that I love you.

So if I could do all this,
And do it in one day.
I would show you all the things,
That words alone can't say.

Lauren Mark

The Mirror Image

I looked into the mirror,
And what did I see?
Someone plain, someone stupid,
The same old, boring me.
But look a but closer,
Through the eyes of the clouds,
And you see someone great,
Of whom you should be proud
No-one dim, no-one strange,
Someone from every day,
No, you see a person unique,
In their own special way.
A reflection,
Just glass upon a frame,
But with a figure
Peering long and hard,
Who thinks they're just the same.
I look into the mirror,
And feel what I can see,
A great and loving person,
Who I know is me.

Maxine Bassett (12)

Harmony

Do not disturb the dew-damp grass,
Fresh and pure,
Pulsating with the Glory of God,
Breathing beauty,
Glistening, glowing,
Generating harmony,
Soothing our discordant lives.
Pause -
And in silent stillness
Soak in this penetrating peace.

Sister St Joseph

Heinz Fifty-Seven

A tower block in the sky
A ready made Haven for misery
Tenants of every nationality
Different as chalk and cheese
Everyone loves their own country
To leave is not by choice always you see
Friction discord apathy

Drug addicts muggers pushers and pimps
Children buying and selling drugs with impunity
As if they were sweets
Radios blaring out you can't hear yourself speak
Children crying in harmony
Who designed these monstrosities

Out for a walk back before dark
Slide the bolts on the front door
Prisoner in flat number thirty-seven
Locked up for the night

An old lady loaded with shopping bags
A young girl with a pushchair
Trundling their way up the stairs
The bleeding lift broke again
Them sodding kids want locking up
It's about time they brought back the birch
A voice outside the lift shouts back
Drop dead you stupid old bat

And look at the state of these bloody walls
Graffiti and filth everywhere
You offer to carry the shopping bags
No you bugger off
The stench and the smell
Of urine on the ground
Hypodermic needles scattered around
The whole bleeding building wants blowing up
To get rid of the muggers pushers drug addicts and pimps

John Moran

A Message For The New Millennium

My dearest daughter how can I say
All that I wish for you today?
A future bright as the golden sun,
Joy, happiness and lots of fun.

May all your days have a glint of gold,
A rainbow in the sky,
That even a dark and dreary day
Will lift your spirits high.

May you have time to stand and dream,
To wander down a lane,
Time to enjoy this beautiful world,
Time to forget all the pain.

Time to watch a skylark soar
Into the Summer sky,
Roses to scent your life's pathway
And friendships that never die.

Beryl Marvin

Granny's Stick

'Granny has gone,' the little boy said as he picked his nose
and scratched his head.
'She didn't say goodbye - not a word - nuffin
I 'spect that's 'cos she was too busy cougin'.
Mum says she's gone to heaven - I don't believe that
'cos heaven has angels and Granny wasn't that.
She was wrinkly and ugly with only one toof, and
a stick she would wave if I didn't tell the troof.
Her glasses were perched on her long beaky nose as
she peered at me through eyes half-closed.
She'd say in a shrill voice wot resembled a bird
'When I was your age kids was seen and not heard.'
and when I was naughty which was *hardly ever!!*
Up would come the stick with a 'Well I never -
in my time you'd have got a clout round the head -
a damned good hiding and sent to bed.'
Still Granny has gone now and I ain't really sorry
'cos now I can play on the stairs with my lorry
without a squeaky shout from the chair where she sat
'You give me a headache - you little brat
and think yourself lucky I'm stuck in this chair - if
I could reach you I'd clip your ear.'
So now Granny's gone I can do as I like
push my little sister off of her trike - tease the budgie
and shout and scream - mix my peanut butter with
strawberry ice-cream - swing on the banisters - give
the puppy a kick.
Oh no!! - here comes Mum with Granny's stick.'

Elsie Francis

The Mill On The Hill

The Mill on the hill stands still.
No more will its big wheel turn.
No sacks of grain on the floor.
No sail on top does turn.

Many years since it is now derelict,
The familiar stone broken;
Split in two and no use any more.
How long is it till it will turn
Again and again and still turn;
Not for many a year to come -
Not for many a year

Justin Bayless

Woodbridge, Suffolk

There natural beauty has been loved and cherished
by all that have lived there.
The River Deben tidal running twelve miles out to sea
to its outlet at Bawdsey, and on to Felixstowe
Transport at the turn of the Century was Thames
Barges. In full sail they were beautiful to see,
Painted often by artist setting on the river bank.
Other barges carried grain to the Tide Mill,
Some with coal, road making materials, and
through the war of 1914-1918 supplies to the troops.
They were unloaded by a team of skilled men
and the term used was called 'running the plank'.
There were smugglers in early history who used
the creeks of the river to unload their loot, which
with the aid of the Parson was stored in the Church.
History more recent on Sutton Hoe they unearthed a ship
which was carried by Captain and Crew to the Burial Ground.
So many fish, birds and wildlife live on the river
and on its banks, so much for nature lovers to see.
There's so much history in this town. The head
of Cromwell was kept in the house of a man
of great regard.
There are lovely chapels and churches, some built
in the 1500s, and pubs with old black beams,
stone floors, and tankards hanging on the walls.

A C Marsh

The Devil's Work

The devil is walking the earth
Causing havoc everywhere he goes,
Trying with all his worth
In the only way he knows.

He tries to make us negative
In everything we do,
Trying to spoil the way we live
Causing wars and famine too.

We must pray to God above
To help us to be strong,
And ask Him for His love
To keep us from doing wrong.

J Bell

The 'Singing' Tree

When I awoke on that morn
It was like being reborn.
Such a feeling of joy was surging through me.
Where had I been in my sleep
Such happiness to reap?
That my heart and soul were joined in harmony.

'Something good was on the way,
Was happening this day,'
An insistent voice was whispering inside,
'It's time now the world to greet,'
So on eager willing feet
I flew from my bed and flung the window wide.

In dawn's luminous half-light
That met my wond'ring sight
All was hushed - yet I sensed something stirred out there.
I couldn't breathe, I hardly dared,
Yet in no way was I prepared
For the magical sound that burst upon the air.

Seemed it was coming from a tree,
For nothing else could I see
And I never before heard such sweet sound,
Was like all the birds of the air
Had gathered up out there
And were singing for the joy of just being around.

How long did I stay so?
I really didn't know.
Can't explain my happening - for I *never* saw a bird,
And yet *something* was there,
Of that I was aware,
And I know what I saw, and I know what I heard.

Daphne Lodge

Let's Get Considerate
(Dedicated to Margaret Kerr and Chris King)

Hail! 21st Century, Here we are!
We Homo-Sapiens have left our scar
On the planet deep. We're too blind to see
The damage we have caused to the earth, wind and sea.

In spacetimes blink of an eye we have raped and pillaged
Mother Nature's crust
And have dumped our toxic spillage
Turning fertile soil to radioactive deadly dust.

We've overrun the planet casting other life forms aside.
Burning down their forests so they have no place to hide.
We've buried hillsides of rubbish, a junkyard in space,
Dump our waste in the sea,
My favourite fish was Salmon and Plaice.
We feed Herbivores waste meat products and treated Shit.
Yum! Yum! What's for Dinner?
Must have one more slice of it.

To the scientist and the farmer
Busy tending the G M Crop,
When the pollen is ready to fly,
You tell the force 9 gale to stop.

Cloning Sheep, Now Humans? What are we to do?
Walking past your brother, was it No 1 or 42?
Certainly brings new meaning to the state of Déjà Vu.
One of me is quite enough. My family think so too.

Spare a thought for Animals, Fish, Birds and Bees for just a tick.
The air that we could breathe and not feel sick.
A sea where we could swim without an oily slick.
And a land where we could tread,
Not hear the Geiger Counters click.

We've made great progress,
And left a trail of debris in our wake
With little thought of implications.
Let's Act Now! For Goodness Sake!

David M Carter

Busy Busy Lives

The small lost soul, hand held out quivering to the sea of people
Riding in new cars, living in nice houses. Bright lights shining in all
of their windows
Busy busy lives
They don't notice him; they have jobs, childrne, husbands, lovers,
wives
Busy busy lives
How strange they cannot hear, never see this small-lost soul
Hand held out quivering and longing, longing just to be a part of
them
One of the sea of people with *busy busy lives*

Jill Florence

Life

It begins with three quarters of a year
Yes, the time is nearly here
Suddenly there is a yell
Can it be a little gel?
Or is it a little boy
Giving someone lots of joy.
I wonder what will be the name
Choosing one, is part of the game.
Years go by and they are five,
Schooldays begin to arrive.
Six to eleven the junior grade
And infant days gradually fade.
Teenage, adolescent and adult
Man and woman is the result.
Boy meets girl, they fall in love
And hope for blessings from above.
Wedding bells ring out and chime
Then it's back to babies every time.
So life goes on until old age
Then we reach the final stage
Of being left all alone
With aches and pains in every bone.
Think of the past for awhile
Surely, one memory will cause a smile.

H M Beresford

View From A Bridge

I watch the lights of London
dance on the river, recall a time
you danced for me;
Busy river, cruising past
Tower Hill, stirring brave
hearts - for good or ill;
As stars flicker like altar candles
and die - river folk
protest not, only I;
Ah, it was not for me you danced!
Nor has the moaning tug below
time for us either;
Wearily, warily, I'll make my way,
let murmuring half-truths
wash over me.

R N Taber

I Dream Of A Beach

Over the beach the sun shines bright,
So bright it's blinding to people's sight,
You feel the golden yellow silky sand,
The same one that burns peoples hands,
Deep blue waves you hear them crashing,
The sheer joy of children splashing,
But wait the vision of the beach it's gone,
What could I have done?
As I go back to reach,
I realise, I dream of a beach.

Anita Patel (14)

Regrets to 2

Tonight I
Met him too late
As one of two men
The other too good for words
But I wanted to
See to them both
Together

S J Flynn

Questions And Answer

I wonder what kind of a wonderful world it would be,
    If *Eve* had not sinned?
    Would we eat from the trees?
    And not know disease?
    And God would we please?
    Adore on our knees?
  If that serpent had not intervened?

I wonder if everyone would love everyone, and war -
    Was something unknown?
    Would we know only trust?
    With kindness a 'must'?
    No knowledge of lust?
    Or returning to dust?
  We'd Worship and obey God alone?

But I fear that the World would be more fearful *now* if Jesus
    Had not come to save.
    Would we still be here?
    Few humans, in fear?
    No life we hold dear?
    No God to be near?
  Would there be no hope beyond the grave?

But we *know* what kind of a world we will go to, as God
    Said He loves us so.
    And in spite of the Fall,
    If we answer His Call
    He'll gather us all
    To His Heavenly Hall,
  Then with our Lord Jesus, we will go.

Hilda Barrett

Untitled

Although you are so far away I feel physically drawn to you still,
Like the magnetism of the poles
Sensations beyond my control continue to rage inside me
I experience momentary loss of control, temporary insanity
I feel I am melting as I dream of your passion
I almost see the fireworks
I hear them as if in surround sound as I drift
I am spinning in the grip of your heart
I float as if suspended in water
Where the safety of your love keeps me warm

In memory I feel the vibrations of your voice
My cheek against your chest
I feel so tiny, engulfed in something much larger than you or I
An understanding without need of voice

I see you in my mind's eye
Bathed in a familiar aura of sensuality
So often I re-live your touch
I gaze into warm chocolate eyes
Laugh, as they shine beneath lashes spun of silk
I see my face reflected, I look so happy
I feel a wild excitement held by an overwhelming sense of calm
Almost a time when water and electricity mix
As if together we can defy the elements

The memory fades to our last moments
The final thought as I watched you walk away
'I have never seen someone in so much pain'
With this I drift into a turbulent sleep, as ever
Until I sleep in your arms again and lie at peace

   C Moon

44

Market Day

The market place
The hundredth face
The stallholders cry
As you walk by

Where's the magic
In the latest gadget
A seller will disown
Once it's found a home

Salt beef or shoes
It's there to choose
The bacon cured as is the cough
At discount price at money off

Parking space is just a curse
When spending wallet or purse
And after you've spent and left the town
The council is there to hose it down

David Thompson

White City Times
(An extract)

Amongst the range
of accumulated clutter
on the mantelpiece
was betting money change:
huge florins, coppers,
compact sixpences and threepenny bits -
too tempting to resist.
Guilty little sinner,
I filched the shining icons,
blewing them on ices, pop and sweets
(instead of nourishing dinner)
down dusty Garford Way,
feeling like a pampered prince,
if only for a day.

Come evening, I would
crouch behind a comic or a book,
caught in the wireless world's
'In Town Tonight',
not keen to catch a look
from he who scanned the race page;
the tension and the brooding
apparent in protruding tongue
at left of lip-stretched mouth
might soon presage a rage.
I feared him then,
but now I know that he too was slave
to mundane life, to poverty,
a woman far beyond his ken,
and dry, seismic smoker's cough
that beckoned him to a peremptory grave.

Wes Ashwell

A Despot Falling

Remember thou art mortal,
Let not my counsel
Fall upon deaf ears.
Man's divinity is bought,
Not with gold and myrrh,
But flesh and blood
And agonising years.

Think not once, but twice or more
Before you utter,
Before a judgement.
The masses won't forgive you,
Not this time I fear,
There'll be no praise
Except a lone lament.

Laszlo Clements

Millennial? No, Timeless!

From a cloudless sky the beautiful sun
scattered its bounty with a loving smile.
Pale-blue heaven met a dark-blue ocean
along horizon that stretched over miles.

Blue met the sand-caressed line of a beach
as the wave fronts rolled on a jutting land.
The afternoon hummed and simmered to reach
our bodies and minds as we sprawled on the sand.

The diffused aura of a high summer
the languorous length of a rapt moment,
pounded our hearts with a passion-hammer
as we lay on the shore by a creek's bend.

The limitless coastline, the boundless sky
the bathers frolicking on golden sands:
the ocean's serenade, a seagull's cry
are woven close in my memory strands.

These moments from my past are truly framed
like portraits brush-worked in a timeless paint.

Shafi Ahmed

A Holiday In Wales

The river flows at Betws-y-Coed
Persistently, finding its way
Around great boulders that lie in its path,
Creating a shining white spray.

It sweeps along over numerous rocks,
Gushing waterfalls large and small
And softly its liquid melody plays,
So soothing the sound of its fall.

The clustering trees provide their cool shade
For those who are out for the day,
To picnic and paddle, walk through the woods
Or rest for a while on the way.

My sister and I have taken the path
From the village, beneath the trees.
She sketches the scene. I sit on a log,
Absorbing the place at my ease.

Observing the river's circling foam,
With the birds singing high above
And some grazing sheep behind us, I feel
That we are surrounded by Love.

Anne Greenhow

Work, Rest And Play

It is Monday again - and a new day is dawning, the same 'old'
routine - it is boring.
I hear the alarm clock ringing in my sleep - to put an end to my
dreams,
now is the time to get my mind and body into motion - it seems.

From my bed I arise - I rub my eyes and scratch my head,
with a yawn and a stretch - my stomach informs me it needs to be
fed.
As I tune into the radio I harken to the voice of Stevie Wonder,
I look out of the window, only to see the rain and hear the thunder.

Now fully awake - washed, dressed and fed I step out onto the street,
I hurry to the station, to catch the train and hopefully get a seat.
Lucky for me I find one - so out comes my book - and on go my
specs,
so private in what I am reading - I can become ignorant of either sex.

Arriving at my place of work - the usual routine of clocking in,
I see telex tape everywhere - on the floor and even in the bin.
The telex and fax have been busy over the weekend,
a good start to Monday, the work piling in so early - is there any
end?

Monday over, my incoming tray with work is still overflowing,
enough is enough, I collect my belongings - too bad I am going.
You see I am off to play badminton at my former place of work,
my partner Annette and I make a good team against Jim and Kirk.

Showered and dressed - I pack up my kit then home I go,
my body aches, my face is red - but oh boy this train goes slow.
Reaching my destination, I stop at the take-away for a chicken curry,
glad to be indoors for I am famished - I eat as though I am in a
hurry.

Feeling much better after having eaten - I turn on the tv
I can watch whatever channel - for there is only me.
My eyes are beginning to close - so off to bed I go,
sleep will soon be upon me - that is something I do know.

Anna Attridge

Century A Brand New Life

A new century at last,
Can we really turn around,
What we did
So wrong in the past.

Now we can do it all
Work together, live together,
No more need
For war or hate.

Can we really do it
Make it all so right,
I wonder if people
Said this before.

Maybe at the
Turn of the last century,
People said and felt
The same.

Can we only hope
We can make it right
Or people will say at
The next century
People didn't care.

E Sheldon

Memories

When I sit alone at home I look at the photos of the past
Memories of my father, the happy times that are so close to my heart.
How I miss him, his lovely smile,
And a happy personality looking at my father's generation and the
Generation of today.
I can see an evil world,
Then I look at the children and I think of their lives, How man is
Destroying the planet polluting the earth, does he really care
About tomorrow or about someone else's pain or sorrow?

Patricia Butler

Ashford (Middlesex)

I'm not an *old* Ashfordian.
We came here in seventy-two
When Ashford,
Was still a village to us.
A village that grew and grew.
So many changes,
Not all for the best,
But, one thing hasn't changed.
Community spirit is living here,
And we are truly blest.
For each shop that I enter,
Is full of friendly folk,
In front, and behind the counter
The finest food, the service great,
And whoever you encounter,
Greets you with a winning smile,
And pass the time of day.
Ashfordians are special,
And in the new millennium,
I really have to say,
I see things still improving
Local folk have pull,
And wouldn't it be something,
To save our local hospital!

Brenda Sohngen

Reality

Sleep my baby close your eyes,
You've had a busy day.
I've cleared up all your soldiers
And put your toys away.

You had a hundred battles
And won them every one,
But baby it's so easy
While you're playing them for fun.

When you grow up to be a man
Your battles are for real.
You cannot put them in a drawer
To hide the way you feel.

I pray you grow up big and strong
My sturdy little land,
And face the future as it comes,
The good times and the bad.

But in the meantime go to sleep
And dream about today.
You're still your mummy's little boy,
Tomorrow is another day.

Molly Thornton

Time Out Of Mind

Old Cairo: the warmth of evening
stretches languorously into night
leaving behind the tumult of the day.

I sit at ease in my darkened room
comforted by the shifting glow of lamplight
and occasional creaks from the wicker chair.
In the corner of the room an ancient clock
ticks tirelessly on defining fleeting moments
binding me to the bollard of the present
but finally I succumb to its quaint mesmerism
and drift away on an ebb-tide
of reflections, reminiscences, forgotten dreams . . .
Gone is the clock, the glowing lamp
the wicker's firm embrace
in this land beyond the weal of time's impress.
When I return it is the clock alone
that challenges the room's sameness:
an hour has fled invisible
but taking with it how many days
. . . and months . . . and years?

Rod Treseder

Jackson Pollock

I saw this exhibition and I'd meant to go
I'd studied long and this was my reward
What met my eye was ecstasy of colour
Surrounded and absorbed by fractal images
I could only wonder and admire
What supreme power creates such energy
At first it seemed like chaos, undefined
But then an order and a purpose grew
And out of chaos came an understanding
A look at life in its primordial shape
The artist knew by instinct how it formed
And dreamed his paintings to reality
Pollock, Jackson Pollock, Jackson Pollock.

Dawn Bishop

Broken Time

Cinnamon
Sticks broken
Over sealing heat
Dip into moist
Memories

Past, present fad
Mingling sounds
On my tongue
Remembering
Feeling
As time ebbs

Slowly unravelling
Spice flows
Through my veins
Travelling
Tasting you

Sue Thakor

The Journey

Our lives are like a journey
Through a day we think can't end,
The morning filled with promise
With hours ahead to spend.

But as we chase the sunlight
The shadows and the showers,
Do we ever stop to heed
The passing of the hours?

We seldom hear the stealthy step
Of evening's gentle tread,
As we watch the sunset's glory
Turn from gold to fiery red.

And as night falls the endless day
Seems but a moment past,
The hopes we had are still but dreams
Our time has gone, alas.

So if your day has just begun
Remember how time flies,
And try to do the things you planned
Before the darkness stills your hand.

William Asprey

Jesus' Love

Jesus' love reaches to all.
The fat, the white,
the black and the tall.

Jesus' love reaches to all.
The rich, the poor,
the sad and the lone.

Jesus' love
Reaches to the high and low
Humble - all.

Jesus' love is pure and strong
It reaches the streets,
and hugs the Avenue Stalls.

It reaches to the dust bin men,
And parks around the 'sinners' quarters,
And to the junkies room,
And sees the hidden tea spoon,

And stretches out to lift you out
If only you would let Him.

Yvonne Sturge-Prince

King Arthur's Fury

'What honey soothes my rage, that hurls
across a jealous noise; what cools
my pride, which chafes my thoughts with rubs?
What peace can throw me to a calmness?
First Guinevere, now Britain's false.

Are they become your prophets now
who roam through pain and suffering,
unclothed, unheard, unknown, unmourned?
We will not feed them with our bodies,
though He who keeps them bleeds for us.

In Anton's house deloused and ulcered,
where songs are strummed at Waterloo
and the whistling jakie beats the bounds
with urine hissing at the rain
by hotel doors' geranium pots

at universities where toads
plop from the mouths of misty men
and atheists, as though their creed
ever converted evil souls,
decline to see Truth serve at tables

and underground in windy lairs
of fiery-nostrilled wormy trains
within those bowels the mass of Man
truncated into carriages
compresses hope and spawns desires

here have I seen that rancid quarrel
between King Uther and good Cornwell.
Pray for the best, prepare for death.
The hues of war intensify.
My arm is heavy with the sword.'

    David Hendtlass

Wash Away

In the midnight stillness, I sit near the sea,
Looking back with my memories of how life used to be.
As the waves crash against the rocks, I remember -
How I thought my life then, no longer did matter.

In my remote sadness I would cry,
As my love, you did not deserve to die.
I had lost you and I did not know what to feel,
How to let you go and when to heal.

I had held you, maybe for a while,
Then I could remember your peaceful smile.
As I look into a burning candle light,
I pray your soul will rest each day and night.

Although it has been sometime I still picture you in my head,
With memories of things I should have done and said.
I know I have to sacrifice our dreams now, for my own -
As I am left with a future - unknown.

As I sit and watch the sunrise on the hearth,
I let my thoughts linger and search.
I see your face as I close my eyes,
To hear you whisper: 'It's time now, this is our goodbye.'

Abida Haidar

Only Seven Days

I only knew
One week of you
But
We loved a lifetime
In those seven days.
And,
All the pain,
Again, again,
I would retrace,
To see your face
That sweet embrace - yet,
I always knew,
One week of you,
Would have to do - my whole life through,
I'd had my lifetime's love
- In only seven days.

   Debra Ingram

The Journey We Take

Shattered dreams lie at my feet
Like tattered rags in a heap
Why did death call at our door?
Why are you with us no more?

The journey that you had to take
Night by night keeps me awake
Where are you? What has become?
Did you simply escape life's humdrum?

The man who with a saintly glow
Helped people live and troubles slow
Was cruelly snatched -
Death dealt its blow

You cured the sick, you filled our hearts
A husband, a father, a man apart
Every day of my life as I recall,
Father dearest you stand tall

I would like to say this to you
The bond we had was real and true
Alone and lonely without you here
But your spirit my father will forever endear.

Seema Khehar

Black Lady Of The Caribbean

Who acknowledged her?
Where is her statue?
Who named her after English towns,
Put her to work in fields, and beat her?
Black lady of the Caribbean;
An unpaid slave of the Empire,
Uncredited for years of service.
She represents all and none of Africa;
Because she was uprooted
From her place of birth,
And sent in chains to work
From dawn 'till dusk, in plantations.
Abused and used by her owners,
Sometimes she gained a Scottish, Chinese, Irish name
And bore children against her will.
When she came to the West
Hollywood cast her in the of nanny, 'mammy', maid,
Comforter and carer of the white woman.
She did this for years too,
Before being given the right to vote.
Then she was put to work as a cleaner,
In the hospitals, in old people's homes;
Caring for those nobody cared for.
Did she not teach us endurance, compassion and charity,
Despite what we did to her?
By her example, she forgave us, with a big heart;
Have we ever respected her,
For all her years of service?
Let's raise her statue high above the Thames in Gold,
With the inscription: 'I made it!' - Such is her story told.

Felicity Kaye

Taking A Back Step

When history
becomes less important

to a need . . .

to love respect tolerate one another
will the Kennwick man mystery?

. . . take a step up.

Mary-Jamuna

Every Woman's Nightmare

It was May of '97
I had a terrible blow,

The Doctor said, 'You've got breast cancer,
The left will have to go.'

I said, 'Oh! Well if that's the case, I'd rather be alive,
anyway the odds are good, and many do survive.'

I had the op and all went well,
Chemo was next to come,

My golden locks all fell out,
my head like a baby's bum.

Then came radiotherapy,
I could relate to a microwave meal,

But all the treatment that I had,
I really didn't feel ill.

The hair's grown back, and looking good,
But I'll never make page three,

My eternal thanks to Guy's Hospital,
for looking after me.

Averil Witherington

My First Day At School

'Mum, why is that girl crying? Is this desk here really mine?
Can I draw pictures with that pencil and what's written on that sign?
When will I have my dinner and where's my Teddy Bear?
You know he's always with me so it doesn't seem quite fair
That when I need him badly, he's not around to see
My classroom and my teacher who's smiling so at me.
Will she help me tie my shoelace for it always comes undone
And will she know I need a biscuit at exactly half past one?

I can't believe you're leaving for I thought you loved me so
And we've always been together in sun, and rain or snow.
And I haven't got a hankie for my face is rather wet
So maybe I'll come home with you. Ted's missing me, I bet!

But look, there's my friend Sally and she wants to come and play
So perhaps I'll stay a little while for there's lots to do today.
There's a book with lovely pictures and a great, big, noisy drum.
Come Sally, sit here by my side. I'll see you later Mum.'

Eileen M Pratt

Millennium Love

A poem for you my love
To tell you of my love
We have had centuries of love
Now we have a millennium of love
Let's just love love
        Love

Kayleigh Darling

People Should Care

He picked his way wearily along the road,
Rejected and homeless, no place of abode.
All day long he had had nothing to eat,
So wet and cold, with no shoes on is feet.

He once did have a job and plenty of food,
A home and family, life was so good.
Along came recession, government to blame,
Redundancy with it, life was never the same.

He heard of a young man in much the same boat,
Who had to sleep out without even a coat.
Then wind and frost came, got to the young fellow,
His legs first turned blue, then slowly to yellow.

It was straight to hospital for him that day,
'Off with his legs,' said the doctor, 'Straight away.'
The first man complained of having nothing to eat,
Till he saw the poor fellow without any feet.

There are many more like him all over the earth,
Refugees having to flee the land of their birth,
From famine, fire, and earthquake, floods and civil war,
Seeking to find others, who'd open their door

To give food and shelter, for people should care,
Those who have plenty should be willing to share,
Especially those who have much all through the year,
The trouble is that many governments interfere.

They try to stop aid getting through to the people,
Bombing homes, schools, even church and steeple
Many of us worry, and most do care,
With those poor people we are willing to share.

But how can we help in their hour of need,
All the lonely and sick, and hungry to feed?
Lord show us the way to get the aid through,
Because You so love them, and we do love You.

Eunice Squire

Past Times

Gone was the field of golden corn,
Gone were the birds in the early dawn
Too noisy now!
No longer to walk the Datchet Way
That belongs to another day
Years ago!
The once sleepy lanes of yesterday, don't exist
Instead, there are rows of buildings
Of grey and motley blue
With hotels and a car park
Instead of a greenery view.
Where once the farmer, ploughed by hand
Gone, are all his fields and land.
Forty-eight acres, that's been sold
In the name of *progress?*
Where the Shire horse walked, down the lane
And the tired plough-boy, lived the same way
Off the life of his ancestors!
Even now, you can hear, the horses' hoofs
With the thatched cottages, is living proof
Of their existence!
Now there's motors, by the score, that
Run down the lane, past the doors
Of yesteryear, a bygone era.
The little stream runs merrily on, but
Now all the people are gone, who lived there.
Plus the trees, and the farm, which
Ne'er did any harm to anybody, all are gone!

   Rosemary Peach

Soaps
(Is Friday night funeral night?)

I watch 'The Street'
    Everyone in floods of tears
Over Judy's sudden death
Follow with a wetter 'Brookside;
    Dear (to some) Greg blown up
    (with a leg over)
What a way to go!
    How the 'Beeb' adores funerals
And buckets of grief
    I'm glad I've only black and white
It suits the mood
    Death is not colourful
It's obscene
    (Greg was not with his wife!)

Bryn Bartlett

The Shelf

A tiny string of blue beads encircles a candle in it's glass holder.
Those beads were your anklet of identity, when you were born.
Next to the candlestick stands a simple wooden giraffe.
You made it when you were at school.
Beside the giraffe, a Prayer plant.
No photographs.

I want to listen to your music, look at your photographs;
But not yet, not now, maybe tomorrow.

I began to write about your life, so filled with achievement,
Disappointment and torment.
I began to paint a picture, trying to capture that look of
Freedom and joy I saw on your face
At the mortuary.

I have not finished these things;
Not yet, not now. Maybe tomorrow.

Anita Meloche

My Wife

A man's best present is his dear wife -
God's choicest gift to cherish all his life;
She is this and that and everything else -
She is the spring that fills life's deepest wells.

She is your air, your water and all you need -
Your friend, guide and philosopher indeed.
She's your baby though she's a full-grown adult
When you face problems, she is ever there to consult.

She is your bread when you're hungry - your drink when you need,
She is cool as a cucumber, yet a gazelle at speed.
She is your pride and joy, your life and soul,
Her absence leaves a huge void - a gaping big hole.

She is your reason for living - all you'll ever want,
With her charm, love and warmth she makes your home a haunt.

My Dina is just one wife with all virtues as above -
A cascade of care, devotion and endless love.
May every happiness, joy and good health come your way -
Today on your Birthday and then day after day!

Soli Master

Into The Millennium

Onward, into the millennium we go -
Will The Year 2000 be greeted with snow?

The New Year brings fresh hopes for all,
We all cheer it in; whether we're small or tall.

Every face will light up, hoping to see
The millennium bring us joy and prosperity.

Also remembering the past; the way we all came
Hoping the future won't be entirely the same.

Parties everywhere, there will be -
Decorated with Millennium Filigree;

And we'll remember the celebrations as we go;
Maybe leaving happy footprints in the New Year snow.

Thinking how the millennium made us all aglow.

Sheryl Williamson

Starlings Over West Pier

The sea surrounds me
Sparkling like a million shards of glass
From south to east in touching these walls
I'm cautiously treading these breezy halls.
Find me on the West Pier
Breathing in this old air
And dancing on salty crystal embers
With Iodine in my hair.
In part of the depths below me
And the starlings towering over my head.
Wailing, crying
While I cling tightly to these rotting beams
That taught me how to love.
My prison mirrors the lights of your modern age
Glancing through dusty broken windows
I see the dazzling splendour
Of a time that leaves me paling
In comparison and wishing that
Once again, I too could be a living soul
In the pit of night
When all modern yellow light has gone
You will leave me here
On this derelict driftwood
With nothing but a modest, pale
Moon to bask under.
The same moon I knew all those years ago . . .
When I first wandered on to the West Pier.

Pippa Beavis

Gifts From God

Thank You, Lord, for the gift of Creation:
For countrysides aflame with golden splendour
As, bounty upon bounty, ten thousand crops ripen,
Yielding plenteous harvests for all to share;
For idyllic fields and open meadows
Where running brooks, fringed with buttercups,
Bathe in oceans of ox-eyed daisies;
And for pastures of deepest emerald green
Lined with hedgerows ablaze with cowslips.

Thank You, Lord, for the gift of nature:
For forest glades echoing to the purest melody
From robin, wren, song thrush and blackbird;
For labyrinths of oaks and hornbeams
Enrobed in mantles of greenery;
And for deepest woodland shades where springs
Arise amidst moss-grown rocks and lawns
Of velvet to form pure crystal streams
Whose curtained cascades, with divinest murmur,
Join in unison with nightingale's refrain -
A falling descant of sublime harmony.

Thank You, Lord, for the gift of Your Son,
Our Lord and Saviour Jesus Christ;
For the love He showed us upon the Cross;
For His Virgin Birth, life, death and Resurrection
To set us free from the bondage of sin;
And for that sweetest gift, Your Holy Spirit -
That wellspring of eternal life,
Arising from Wisdom's sacred fount
And flowing through us like a crystal stream
Now and for evermore.

Robert D Hayward

Tophet

blind watch
from the foetid hollows of the dovecote
mansions crammed
that smell of sex and death
grass grows yellow
in the damp shadow of the methadoned horses
moon-eyed
trembling with the megrims
drag another
spent fetish
to the bonfire

Nicholas Johnston

Last Walk

A walk through the forest,
Peace, smell of old wood,
Dark earth grinding beneath your foot,
The sky can't be seen for branches and leaves
Still, it is summertime
Enjoy it, and breathe
Go back to nature, forget your grief
To be as one with earth and sky,
It feels like coming home.
Say your farewell to a dear one, you knew,
Say it outside, without walls,
Let your feeling pour out of you.
To make you well, once more,
Forgive yourself, for the errors, you made
Stop blaming yourself,
We are all made of the same,
Be honest to others and kind and understanding,
Not being honest, can cause so much pain,
To you and others on this vast plain
A walk through the forest
Will really do you good.
I hope this will be my resting place
To lay under trees, when my time comes,
Seen those white robes flowing
On people I have once known
A very very long time ago,
Sleep well, I will never forget you.

Heike Jardine

What Should We Believe?

What does shelter really mean?
Is it just a passing dream
Designed to fool those who are old
To make them do as they are told?
But some old people see through mist
They understand they're on a list
And much depends on those in charge
Will he or she your faults enlarge?
Do we believe in all we hear
Or do we push away this fear
And give the scientists a shove
Who say it's through the nose we love
Because two small blobs sit and sniff
Until they find a similar whiff?
Just don't believe in all you hear
For if you do then you've gone queer.
Believe in God who'll put things right
Despite the fact He's not in sight.

Mary Carr

River

Slender river
soundless your water,
undivided, flowing continuous
waves rush against rocks
creating white foamy bubbles.

where are you from?
Are you from the mountain
      of the north
where white snows are there,
flowing and dancing
like a carefree goddess,
unattached to worldly things.
You look like a heavenly maiden
      looking for a lover.

Bright lights coming
      from darkness
reflecting, shining
      on the water.
Sun, moon and stars' shadows
      twinkle on you.

You are clean and pure
you don't look back
      destroy whatever comes your way
      Don't pick them
      Don't store them.
You have no grief
      no fear,
Just flowing and rejoicing.

Suti Sen

If

If you should die Most Beloved
Would I not take my truth
Wherever I would have to be
And hold it tight against my heart
Like a small urn with your ashes?

If you should die Most Beloved
If your soul would go before I
Would I therefore not also die
Close my heart my lips for life
Keep safe and sealed the mystery?

If I your Beloved should die
No one but you should know
The accomplishments of our souls
How we tried to serve the truth
Finding it oft though not always

Let us live now Most Beloved
Let us protect our very breath
We have for better and for worse
Entwined the music of our souls
Amidst the sacred sound of Life

Marianne Harvey

Two Minds

Two people encapsulated -
in time capsules -
of their own making -
both 'doing, 'speaking' and 'saying' -
within the boundaries - laid -
with all looking in -
except maybe, to the perceptive eye
of you or I -
where all things met
in the elements of time
and all feelings become one
in the blink of an eye

Jane Sander

Sing To It

As time goes on, so does life
Every day brings new forms of happiness and sadness
Though the sun continues to shine
Stars flicker in the night sky
Birds sing as beautiful as ever
Wolves howl to the moon like the generations before them

However
Once every eighteen months, an extraordinary thing occurs
Somewhere in the world a magical event takes place
It has ended wars and brought people together
People fear it, worship it and sing to it

This event is the Eclipse
An event that brings countries, towns and cities to a halt
Birds go silent
Street lights flicker
As the moon kisses the sun

For a few minutes, day becomes night
Everything goes silent
People stop and casually look up as the moon glides in front of
The sun

What a sight
A wonderful, natural event has just occurred

Mark Solomons

Choral Evensong

Out of so many throats, the music soars
In high crescendos, touching wood and cold
   grey stone
With arcs of sound.
Cassocks of red and white sway as one,
Cocooned in light beneath the organ's swell.
Beyond is darkness softly closing round
Pillar and pew.
Time has an edge on beauty, soon too soon
   the music and the voices fade,
Slip into silence.
Now in a slow procession, wordless figures move
Out of the light,
Are folded up at last
In cloaks of darkness. Shadows throng.
The organ throbs its final note,
Shudders once more, is still.
Weathered and worn through centuries, this wood
And stone stand proud and dignified
Out of an English earth.

   Elizabeth Ryeburn-Gilchrist

A Cry For Help

Somebody help me!
I am so lonely
I can hardly bare it.

My heart is empty
My soul is dead

I am forever condemned
To a living death.

What have I done so wrong
That I stay alone so long.

Cursed I am for the wrong I have not done.

Who do you turn to
When the going gets tough
If God won't help you
Then life is rough.
You may say this is blasphemy.

But I'm afraid this is the way life has turned me

Sara Coelho

Was This All A Dream?

There is a hush and stillness never known before
The silence is quiet deafening as we sense it more and more
Some great happening has occurred were we not aware
As in this silent episode I wonder who will care?

Prolonged remains this calm and tranquillity beholds
There is no noise of every day life all is old and cold
The hush is like a coverlet that wishes to remain and keep
Those treasured golden dew drops as we are lulled to sleep

No noise in this reality no noise why should we care?
All had been alerted and like statues now appear
Life has been stopped momentarily for us we ask why?
There is a worldwide census performed by angels on high

Each allotted to a task as slowly all is restored
None knew of this holy predicament none could be ignored
Approaching a holy member I then questioned why?
He produced a variety of parchments and two thousand years
were not denied

When all had been completed he suggested I accompanied him along
Amidst the host of many angels and their plaintive songs
Clouds parted to reveal as a brighter light appeared
Two thousand had gained it's place on earth despite those many fears

I was set down and tired I became and soon sleep enfolded
I heard the babbling of a brook and birds that scolded
Awaking to this reality to the present hum drum and noise
Surely I had not been dreaming? As two thousand was enthorned
and the truth enjoyed

R D Hiscoke

At School In The 1930s

I think that teaching has improved
    Since I attended class,
For place in higher school I had
    Eleven-plus to pass.

Each year we had an Empire Day
    And sang 'God Save The King'.
For our loved ones, sick and dying,
    There were no songs to sing.

We had Scripture in our classes
    And prayers were said each morn.
But teacher never told us how
    A human child was born.

They said Nelson was a hero
    And Britain ruled the waves:
But failed to mention fortunes made
    By merchants trading slaves.

They told us of great battles won:
    Trafalgar, Waterloo.
They forgot the Peasants Revolt
    And left out Peterloo.

They taught us Shakespeare, Tennyson.
    No Darwin, Marx or Freud.
Or those many famous writers
    That I have since enjoyed.

When I turn back the clock I find
    Praise is due, with hindsight.
My teacher taught me how to count
    And how to read and write.

F G Ward

Sculpture And Poetry

The craftsman's panoramic scale
Is a work of sculpture's outer form
And inner tensions that subtly prevail
Are the true artist's graphic norm;
Where the sculptor's art in a poetic frame
Creates a unity of truth and beauty rare,
Its logic is transformed in art's creative name
From a sense of duty clear:

Captured in febrile bronze or nervous stone
Subtle like a poet's rhymes
Evoked; to loving ingenuity prone,
With a power to conjure at all times
With spatial symbols in polarity;
Wrought from a habit of experience,
Its mien shining infinite and free
In full glory to honour love's magnificence:

Words in imagination's space
The poet sculpts giving the phrase solidity
In a context of the human race,
Words that glow with power in their capacity
To build strong towers of feeling,
A warrant to true fame,
One art from the other subtly stealing,
Yet both essentially the same.

Angus Richmond

A Miracle I Wish We Could All Share

A woman came up to me today
Placed her hand on my pregnant belly
Almost time now I said as excitement was
Brimming from my whole being
As I looked into her eyes I felt as though
I was almost drowning in the sadness that I saw there
Like a black hole ready to swallow me
As the baby moves a smile twitches
At the corners of her mouth
Not quite reaching her eyes
Eventually she speaks, her words
Like a hot poker searing through my heart
'I would give anything to have a bump like yours'
As I walk away sadness fills my heart
Wishing that every woman could enjoy
The wonderful experience of motherhood.

Samantha Vaughan

Second Sight

To have it all but see it fade away,
To be afraid of every passing car
And to look up and not perceive a star
Is awful. As the world becomes more grey
It snarls at you; you are now its prey.
You feel despair that used to be so far
Creep nearer. Everything seems lost bar
One ray of hope, one little shining ray.
And then a ward, doctors in stiff grey coats,
Bright lights and lancets, peace and night . . .
White-coated doctor greets you with a smile,
The room is full of colours, rays and spots
As you thank God for the new gift of sight
Frightened to close your eyes, even for a while.

A Nicol

Richmond Park

Richmond Park upon the hill
A part of England living still,
In an age when country walks,
Were not just part of people's talks
Of things they knew when they were young,
With England's beauties praises sung.
God Almighty has an eye
For all things lovely that is why
He has allowed us still to keep
The glades where Spanish bluebells sleep;
Watch your feet for rabbit holes;
A place for pure and simple souls.
Who just love peace and health and life,
Away from greed and hate and strife.
To see the deer like statues standing,
And by the lake the heron landing;
People let their dogs run free,
And squirrels are a sight to see.
The Isabella Gardens make
A lovely sight quite near the lake.
A beauty spot like this should be
Here for all eternity.

Mary Crowhurst

The Approach Of Winter

When I was young I climbed trees,
for apples, plums, and pears.
Now I get out of breath,
just walking up the stairs.

Things that I enjoyed doing,
like cycling, and swimming.
I still think I can do them now,
who do I think I am kidding.

Before I learned to walk,
mum pushed me in my pram.
Now I have a wheelchair,
my wife gets me to where I am.

Long have I been retired,
the rat race and the strife.
A lucky man to have,
a great family and a lovely wife.

I have four super grandchildren,
who keep me from feeling old.
But one thing's for sure,
in winter I do feel the cold.

Bill Dawson

Time To Say I'm Sorry

I thought I'd write to you this note
Although it may leave a lump in your throat
An apology I feel is owed to you
For my younger days and the things I'd do

When in my years as a teenager
Often into trouble I would wander
For I was far from being sweet and innocent
I behaved so bad the devil's child to you was sent

Whether at home or at school
It was me who would break every rule
Regardless of the consequences, for I just didn't care
Unfortunately I can't turn back time
So to my past I bid 'Auld Lang Syne'

But before I can do this, I want you to know
I realise the pain I caused, hurt you so
And your love for me I did underestimate
Thinking the atmosphere between us was filled with hate

To you I now want to apologise
Before you to rest in heaven's skies
This note I sent to mum with a dove
But with you in person, I now share my love

Pam Culverhouse

The Betrayal

Like an arrow his words her heart he hath pierced, her head she
hung wounded by his words. From him she fled, no shoes on her feet
as on and on she ran with his words echoing in her head like a song.
She knew not when or how she happened upon the stream, she felt
not the icy waters as it pulled her to its bosom, no scream or sound
did she utter as death she willingly embraced. Her life before her eyes
flashed as she saw him then on that summer's morn when he had
smiled at her. At that moment she had no presentiment of his betrayal
of her love for him. She gave to him all her innocence and he took it
with arms open wide.

She loved him then and she loved him now as from her the stream
her life ebbed. She remembered too the rising sun on their faces as
the dawn they eagerly awaited that summer's morn and the promises
he made to her. She thought she heard his voice begging her
forgiveness, his face she thought she saw as her last breath she drew.
It was over, she will sleep for evermore and the world of men she
leaves behind, will he mourn her! Or will he fly to the arms of his
other love!

From the stream they pulled her, a smile on her face they beheld as if
she was victorious; she was beyond the hurt of men. Her lifeless body
to the church in the village they carried and there they laid her to
rest. What of her lover now? What pain does he feel? What anguish
is his heart to bear? Her life she sacrificed and in his heart she will
forever dwell!

Deborah Cole-Jordan

Memories

Memories good or bad they will always stay with you,
Some you would very much like to forget, but they still hang around
no matter what you do.
Some memories, the nice ones bring back pleasure and so much
happy times you recall,
Remember that old 'Ford Eight', that was very noisy and was inclined
to stall
But you also remember the bad memories for they are the ones that
stay with you longest of all,
For they bring back sadness and so many, many regrets.
They are indeed the sort of memories that your mind won't let you
forget.
But not all memories are in the mind,
There is another sort, look into that photo album and you will find,
So many joyful memories of people and days long passed,
And just like the mind memories, they will of course last and last.
So would it be better if we had no memories good or bad
I think myself that if that were the case, it would be very sad,
And on reflection would be most unjust,
For memories make life worth living and they really are a must.

A E Reynolds

New Millennium Hope

I wish that I could share with you
    the hope within my heart
A world where peace and happiness
    are covering every part

To stand upon a hill top high
    with you by my side
Stunned by beauty all around
    spread out so far and wide

Walking through a leafy wood
    where children's play is free
When fear and pain and suffering
    are just a memory

Together with all wickedness
    now something of the past
So we can live a full rich life
    forever, now to last

With all our friends around us
    we can trust implicitly
No more war to come between us now
    we live in unity

I do not see a mirage
    nor am I living in my dreams
Though to the vast majority
    I know that's how it seems

No you have had a glimpse into
    the way the world should be
If only for a moment
    shared the hope inside of me

Julie Willis

What Is A Grandson?

A grandson is a special little bundle of joy
Who grows very quickly, into a mischievous little boy
He will come out with a very good wisecrack
And is never too slow in answering you back

A grandson is someone who gives you so much pleasure
He is the little boy, who memories you will always treasure
He is the little fella, who falls and cuts his knee
And will often phone you up, and ask to come to tea

Then you cry the first day he starts the nursery
One minute he's born, before you know it, he's turned three
And then he is a boy cub, before long he is a scout
He gives you all his drawings, that's what it's all about

Then he starts to play football, that is a real man's game
He says he likes a team, but he don't know its name
He will try to remember, with all of his might
But all that he knows is, their colour is blue and white

His daddy will drum it into him, that 'Chelsea' is their name
And if he wants to take up sport, then football is the game
We know that this is really a very special little lad
For he is our third grandson, and our son is his dad

Beryl Horne

Paranoia

She says her name is Paranoia.
Everyone is out to get her.
She's a twisted little vixen.
Say hello to Paranoia.

A master of disguise.
Smiling face hides treacherous eyes.
Insidious soul the dye is cast
She begins her trick.

Like a magician she spins her lies.
Turns them into truth before your eyes.
A skilled manipulator.
Candy coated deceiver.
Duplicitous fabrication burns anguish in my heart.

I lament the day I met you.
For sorrow is all you have brought.
One day you will receive your nemesis for all the hurt, pain, grief
And misery you have caused.

A Holness

Wispy Love

When the skies are this blue
all seems possible for me
and you.

When the night is this still
nothing can fulfil me
like you do.

And, when you look for
me,
where will I be?

Looking for you,
where I always do

up there
    without a care
        in the world.

Nathalie Duval

A Long Way From Home

A slow moving river reflects
An image of a place I knew
The distant fisher casts a line
With no hope of a catch

My thoughts mull around
So many wasted opportunities
I am another distant fisher
Who would net a reflection

Yet these clumsy hands create
Mere ripples on the mirror
Causing one more child to cry
A long way from home

I sleep, tho' dreams give no rest
The guilt awaits another morning
Scant hiding place under this star
Is this our long threatened hell

Paradise without a moments peace
A reflection appearing to mock
Everlasting reminders of our lives
Lived with undue care for self

No holy day here to repent
Just eternity left to ponder
On the wrong road leading
To a long way from home

John Marshall

Spirits Of The Dawn

Come to me, redeeming, you wild sweet passioned air.
Wash away the pain - the hurt inside.
Take me back. Return my memory to where
The days were lifetimes long. The nights denied.

Speak to me, unburden, you anthology of verse.
Let my heart encounter, in your lines,
All that was discovered on the pages you disperse.
All that was directed by your signs.

Call to me, proclaiming, you dignity and pride.
Lift me on your shoulders - raise me high!
Give me back tomorrow. Let the past be satisfied.
Release me from the shackles of your tie.

Reach to me, undying, you spirits of the dawn.
Break the spell, cut the enchanted cord.
Leave me, with your angels' kiss, your promises forlorn.
Free me from your beauty never flawed.

   Robert Springle

Survival Of The Biggest

Awe-stricken like a trusting idiot
Bawling cavalier caterwauls the child
Disturbed from angelic sleep with a lot
Of dismal round headed judgement, beguiled.
Through eyelids of demi-onion slices
In turgid beetroot shell sucks acute sense
Trap doors open, transcending all prices -
Crimson indignation of innocence.

Home work! Hurry! An academic thrill
Of examination preparation
Techniques. But somewhere lost within the drill
Inalienable right to freedom
Of thought is dismissed as ignorance through
Regurgitation of standard textbook
Formulae - because Daddy said: 'Go to
The Knowledge College.' Stalemate by rook.

If in some intellectual pursuit
Of recognition for intelligence
You too could centrifugally exude
Such as sense of need in the present tense
As you centripetally absorb the
Platitudes of great masters, receptive
To none that do not have tradition of
Time on their side, my friend, you would not give
Quite such a stamp of approval to those
Adults anxious with their own ambitions
That dare to feed the child on fragile hopes
With the weary excuse: But Darwin said . . .

K R Plumb

Angel Dust

Angel, when you come to me,
I feel free to roam and float.
On your wings I glide with you,
through peace and silent hope.

You open up a world to me,
with eyes much wiser than others.
You share your soul with openness,
nothing to hide and nothing to fear.

Your translucent fragility does not lie,
and you move with grace and beauty.
Please dance with me my angel,
and protect with warmth and solace.

Show me beyond mans vision,
the nature of your life.
Memories of travel, etched forever
in your mind.

The affinity you have with us,
never lets you down.
You guide me well my friend
now you must go to others . . .

Karen Roberts

New Year's Day

New Year comes round every year,
Bringing with it season's cheer,
Every year fresh hope it brings,
Of better luck with the new Springs.

Families have a New Year Party,
With dancing, music, greetings hearty,
Ring out the old, ring in the new,
Wishes for a good year too.

New Year's the time for resolutions,
Hearing of change and revolutions,
Summer holidays to plan,
Hopes for a better life for Man.

New Year's a time for concerts and plays,
Films, circuses, cartoons for holidays,
New Year's a time for dancing and laughter,
For wishes and hopes of better times ever after.

Susan Mary Robertson

Eternal Misanthrope

Father Time,
Be not such a miser,
I know I cannot escape your clutches.
I know your atrocities have reigned
Even before antediluvian times.
I know from Adam till today,
Is only but a moment
In your grand calendar.
I know that I am
With all my frailty, indulging,
In an anachronistic resurrection.
But surely Old man,
I do not ask,
Our of your treasures of eternity,
Epochs or eras.
Neither do I ask you
To stitch up my lacerated soul.
Nor do I ask you
To slacken these ever tightening
Boa constrictors of your hands.
All I ask
Are a few split seconds,
And the moments needed
For one flickering of my lashes,
Enough for freezing still
The kaleidoscopic cascade
Of that lovely beauteous sight
On the canvas of my mind.
That is all I ask of you,
And that too only once in a while.

Sophia Ahmed

Alone With My Reflections

Alone with my reflections,
I looked across the years, and
Remembered as a child there was never any fears, I
Would be sent to the shops, and played in the streets
Played on the river banks any day of the week
With handfuls of bluebells gathered near the trees,
Would look for the butterflies, but avoid the bees
Now a pensioner, times have changed, people do not care
We cannot unlock our doors or go anywhere,
The respect has gone, and fear echoes people's hate
Some feeling beyond my understanding, and my mind awakes,
I looked in another direction but it was me,
I yawned and looked at the image there to see,
My face a little wrinkled and my eyes evolved with
The uneasy seventy-three pee extra I had to solve,
We must urge our government harder to try as
This is an insult really, what can we buy?
But God will bless our New Millennium this we are sure,
With good health, peace and unity as in the days of yore.

M Joseph

Correction Of Desire

A correction of a praying child,
Leaves desire to fate.
Like a heart pounding in repetition,
And a baby born late.

I dwell in a place called peace,
It keeps the outside tame.
You hunt for a life of peace,
But you turn in the wrong lane.

Cradle in one's arms,
The pumping blood on a thorns tip.
Let it seep through a darkened moon,
Like a tap all ready to drip.

I curl as new born dream,
I step in line then fall on stream.
Desire has to hold the key,
For love and happiness to finally see:
Each Correction you Pursue.

Lisa Watts (16)

The Outing

Dusk falls in the stalls
Shirty, flirty
Cruising for something dirty
Down among the rent boys
Cast aside the decoys
That's put 'em off the scent, boys
Hallo, sailor
Here comes Akela

High class, top brass
Can pay for something flashy, trashy
Or maybe something weedy
In toilets really seedy
Mater's little hero
Acts like bloody Nero
Down among the rent boys
Here comes Akela

Then a scrub at the club
Rub-a-dub
To soap away the smell
So no-one's going to tell
And to glory in the shower
In the naughty, secret power
Of having bought the fear
Of 'some bleeding little queer'
Here comes Akela

Key in door, what a bore
Got to lie a little more
It's hard, this façade:
Nice life
Charming wife
Sterling chap -
Full of crap -
Just for mother
It'd nail her
Here comes Akela

Lorna Todd

Looking Out

My friend it's important to you
    to look forward to the great change in our decade.
That day is one for all mankind
    especially those in the Christian kingdom.
The millennium they call it
    The year 2000 to all
        The 21st Century is almost upon us now.

I'm looking our for Jesus Christ
    I don't know when He'll appear.
        The signs are foretelling and reeling like a film.

Christ mentioned his preparation for us
    of mansions in the sky
        He prayed a prayer to keep us from the enemy at large.

Matthew 24 and 25 sets the scene to come
    the men who call themselves the Christ
        with revolutions on their mind.
They trick the people to join them
    to set apart themselves
        to dwell in isolation and give up all their wealth.

The children of today have changed,
    the ones who go to school
        are roaming with knives and guns and threatening all around.
All kinds of weapons are passing through their hands,
    the violence rises up and no one is in control.

But on one magnificent day to come
    The sky will unfold,
        the trumpet will sound

Then those who hear the majestic sound will rise to meet their
                    Saviour in the sky.

Dionne McLean

A Woman To A Man

I like my freedom, but I want you.
Seldom do I feel more intensely
than when I see your manly features
I need a man, as part of my liberty.

Emotional objective of my soul
is to get, what I want to give,
passion born out of mutual attraction
that yearns for physical connection.

I have loved more than once
so I know the level of my intensity,
towards you I am drawn like a magnet
that wants to stick to your manhood.

Time has taught me, if I don't make a move
we both might lose, hard to find
fragments of sweetness in our daily life.

Can I awake in you, your hidden pride
that as a man, you can make a woman
feel, the way she wants to.

Silvia Kufner

Rye

This sea-wrought town that's stranded like a whale
enshrines soft hill and gazes on beached port
with pebbled streets, warehouses and Kings' fort
defending power whose strength filled traders' sail.
Beyond the walls reclines a sheep-grazed vale
(framed by canals and modest dune resort)
where wool is sheared and happiness is sought
in ancient chapel or strong country ale.

Both close and far, it calls a mermaid song
enchanting artist's hand and bearded sage
And draws a place where one can still belong
while town church clock chimes out a timeless age
when faith prevailed and lion-hearts were strong
protecting from east wind and channel's rage.

Francis Pettitt

At Night

There's just the cat and me,
Alone together at night,
I've pulled the curtains tight,
So no one can peer through,
And give me a sudden fright.
It's different now:
In the stillness of the night,
Except for a passing car,
Heard, but not in sight.
Another day has been and gone,
Never to return,
Tomorrow is another day,
Which we *all* have lessons to learn.
For our lives consist of 'notches',
Knocked of 'our slates', each day,
Our cards, are marked by 'He' who watches,
We thank You Lord,
For the precious time, You graciously allow us,
In every single way!

Jackie Stamford

Dawn Awakening

As I lay waking in the dawn,
My mind began to stir,
My thoughts were all at once
So vivid and so clear.
Your image came so close to me,
You might have been right there.
As all the things we do and say
Came flooding back to me,
My mind was full of happiness,
Of things I treasure dear.
Such as how I love it when
You come to me in need,
The joy I find in helping you
Giving comfort when I can,
Of how my understanding is
So easy, from me to you to give.
Of how I have no shame
In wanting you in love.
How pride swells up within me
To have you close beside
To see you talk to others
And know that they too see
Your beauty and your gentleness
Which are so clear to me.
My thoughts you see were full of you,
A wondrous thing for me
To start the day with happiness
And knowing you are near.

   C R E Peirce

The Stones Speak
(For Paddy Heaney - 'Pilgrim in the search for truth . . . ')

Etched in stone
The story of a people told.
Of land conquered
By a Viking band.
Of Celts who travelled
And with hand, tilled and carved
Raised in stone
Monuments for all who roam
This secret land.
Soil upturned
Reveals the story of a people - old.
Silent voices speak from graves
Neglected down centuries of time.
And now rise up, a resurrection anew
Of ancient names.
Of peoples, kin,
To all who dwell within
This land of Gaels.
Footsteps on the stones of time,
Carve out a path, that leads us all,
Pilgrims, in our search for truth
That roots us to this mystic place.
Spirits of the underworld
Touch our souls
Talk in stone
Cry out with pride
To us of peoples: wise in word,
In craft, in skills and
Cloaked by the surrounding hills
Of Erin.

Olive Carroll

By A Lochside

Born of a glacier gliding
over the rugged land -
four hundred million years
of carving with a loving hand -
the lochs grace Bonny Scotland,
shining ribbons long and wide;
and these extend still further
to rivers like the Clyde.
By mountain streams purling yonder,
the Highland cattle graze,
while mountains like Ben Nevis
look on in silent gaze.
Roads serpent through misty heather,
shepherds tend their wandering flock
come sunshine, or inclement weather,
as I sit watching, on this rock.
My eyes contemplate Loch Lomond,
as once they did Loch Ness -
and I dream of the wondrous story
told me by my old nurse Bess.
I once thought I saw Nessie;
maybe my eyes did me deceive.
How I longed to see her.
In her I did believe.
Sitting by the loch with a seagull by my side,
were I a Scottish maiden
my heart would swell with pride.

   Fuchsia Coles

Innocent Ignorance

She falls,
Almost as if someone had told the world to stop spinning,
Crying children and screaming voices,
All reduced to distant murmurs,
The eerie silence confused with their pleas,
So many visions of pain and suffering,
Which had been all too vivid for her innocent eyes,
All faded to a murky blur.

She reaches out to touch their frail and skeletal hands,
They are weary, defenceless, too tired to cry out,
They will her to help them,
To glance their way and understand their pain,
Their looks are like torture to her,
Their eyes glare back into her own,
And yet they look past her, through her,
To another world far beyond them,
They have stopped hoping.

She begins to cry,
Her tears are wet,
Like rain to a dying tree,
It makes her stronger, she is real,
But so are the children whose empty gazes are engraved in her mind,
Even when she closes her eyes,
Their hands appear to her,
Reaching out through the blackness,
Helplessly hanging on to the fragments of hope,
Which had been torn away from their lives,
Snatched from them so quickly that happiness remains only as a
                                                        memory,
Holding on for the day when someone will start their world spinning
                                                        again.

Mariko Ollason (14)

119

The Needle

You wouldn't know it to look at me, at a glance nobody can tell.
There are no outward signs that mark or distinguish me.
The raiment-wrapped hide covers up a needle-jabbed surface,
And my garments relate no symptoms nor offer any diagnosis.
I appear as real and as seemingly the same as do the well.
I am badged with no brand or insignia that names me.
I live as well as I can, coping as others just like me.

My drug of choice; cigarettes and coffee, first thing every day.
For the sharps-box in the refrigerator below stairs, I reach inside
Habitually for my works, and then shake the phial of semen-hued
fluid.
Stirring up the clouds aiming for the correct consistency.
Unfastening the white plastic hood of the plunger
Unsheathing the orange scabbard of the spike, piercing
And puncturing the inverted tube and so filling the syringe.
Make quite sure to measure out the proper dose.
As focused as a sharp-shooting sniper locked on target, avoiding
Air bubbles, forced free with finger-tip dextrous flicks.
Somewhere, on the dartboard of my skin I choose a suitable site to
shoot.
That soft submissive subcutaneous target, shoulder, stomach, thigh or
buttock
Injection. The first of two today as every single day. Unmissable.
The sting of cold metal sometimes, or even a winking bubble of blood.
Later a yellow bruise appears as witness with testimony of mauled
muscle.

I have to repair to the cubicle in a toilet, just like a junkie.
When I have a social function to attend, the sight of me may offend.
Injecting, jacking up a shot, alone to perform this vital ritual.
It maintains my life, I must be, nothing other than careful.
This is my condition and it sets me apart making me different.
Neglect would ultimately lead to coma, or sometimes hypoglycaemia.

That inebriated-like state; unnatural sweat, tremors and disorientation
Confusion, panic, self-loathing and humiliating embarrassment.
I could be worse off, with some publicly profiled ill; Cancer, Aids or
Epilepsy.
Indeed I could be a junkie; I possess the tools, and as a breed we do
share
At least twice daily, injections dispensed through a flesh stabbing
needle
Apparatus that is with me always, balancing an existence threatened
and short.
Ahead, life truncated but fully enjoyed, not needleless but
nonetheless.

Martin Snasdell

Love Me Once Again

Touch me with your finger tips.
Walk with me in the rain.
Make me feel the world is mine
And our time has come again.

Set the clock for yesterday
And take away the years.
Come, give me back my youth,
And wash away the fears.

Oh, hold me in your gentle arms
And tell me you are mine.
And say you love me once again,
And we'll be together for all time.

Elaine Setohy

Only Wish

Now I am sat here feeling lonely and all I wish for is your return - if
                                                                      only
You would do me the favour of still wishing to savour
The taste of my lips. I miss you, my sanity flips
At the mention of your name.
I wish I thought you felt the same
Because at least then I could send
My thoughts and know that they are yours as well
But I feel isolated in unreciprocated hell.
So my worries are etched upon my face
And while externally I accept the split with good grace,
Internally I am still stuck in our life together
And what makes it worse is that I know you will never
Make the same mistake again.
Right now I am clinging on to 'us' as friends.
I thought we'd never end. How little I knew!
So when from my life you withdrew your love and support,
Did you wonder if anything caught me on the way down?
I remain submerged in love. Just wishing my heart would let me
                                                                    drown.

Iain Henley

British Isles 2000

Four peoples, each with cultural reserves.
Do they enjoy getting on each other's nerves?
The Welsh beneath the rain, liking fudge and toffee.
The English, turned from love of tea to coffee.
The Scots, so quickly reached when trains take half the time,
Blaming the English for bringing drugs and crime.
Say nothing of the Irish, simply pray.
Will they cease the pain one blessed day?

Joanna MacKay

The Millennium Bug

It isn't round
It isn't square
Not on the ground
Nor in the air
What is it?

It can't be touched
It can't be seen
It can't be felt
What can it mean?
How can it be in my machine?

It has no legs
Not even wings
It has no tail
Yet they say it stings!

I still haven't found it
There was such a to do
Perhaps after all this
It died from the flu!

Janice Brooks

Growing Age Of Crime

In the Fifties, when I was young, I could walk free.
I didn't need my mum with me.
If I wanted to think, and be alone
I could walk for miles all on my own.
I could go blue belling, tadpoleing or fishing with a net and jar,
or blackberrying while walking near or far.
I could take a picnic and find a nice site
and stay there all day, returning at night.
And as I grew up I travelled far and wide,
didn't think twice about a train or bus ride.
I went out into the countryside and to sea,
never felt or heard the word hostility.
In the Seventies I had children of my own, a daughter and a son,
I took them many places, we had such fun.
But now in the Nineties, I think twice,
as the big outdoors isn't as nice.
Even going to the shops brings some fear,
you hold on to your purse in case there's a mugger near.
And when you go on a bus or take a train ride
there could be a knife-man sitting at your side.
If you're white, in the eyes of a coloured man that's wrong.
If you're coloured, with the white people you don't belong.
There's child abuse, and bombs exploding,
there's people with guns, bullets they are loading.
You're not even safe in your care in this day and age,
as now there's a new form of violence called Road Rage.
Things are getting worse, this really bothers me.
Is this the world in which my future grandchildren are going to be?

M I Goodwin

In Salute Of The Third Millennium

May mankind thoughts of the Millennium be golden,
And of all minds and hearts that manifest gladness,
As they sing joyfully, Christ's hymns of happiness,
As blessings will arrive upon them now and then.

Yet may mankind salute with open hearts Thy Name,
And always will accept Thy Saviour's Fame,
And give pledge that we will cherish the life's faith,
Aim to delight Jesus Christ at the Heaven's gate.

For His Glory give our life always voluntary,
And too, with whom we share our daily earthly life,
And trod on the path with love's acclamatory,
For other Universe study the books of Light.

There must be the Almighty who has power,
Upon the golden clouds that hold Thy Command,
That had affected our life 'nd our behaviour,
Which comes fair upon our life by move of His hand.

And let us turn head up and speak to our own soul,
And go with open hearts to face the human race,
And with poor and sick within this delightful World,
With the life that comes and beholds Christian grace.

Milan Trubarac

127

Just A Little Boy

I'm just a little boy
I think I'm six or seven
I'm hungry and I'm lonely
My mummy's gone to heaven

The soldiers took my daddy
and killed my little brother
There's fighting in the street now
so I must run for cover

The day they killed my mummy
I cried and cried and cried
And then I looked around me
for somewhere I could hide

I'm nobody's little boy now
I think I'm six or seven
So hungry and so lonely
won't someone care for me

There's different soldiers here now
they're kinder but they're tough
The bad men all have run away
I think they've had enough

I'm hungry and I'm lonely
won't someone care for me
I won't be any trouble
just hug me and feed me

Louis Robert Early

My Time

Father forgive these men
they know not what they do.
They beat me and crush me
and drive nails through.
Their insults lash, like strikes from a whip
broken is my body; yet I cannot give in
You cannot take this cup from me
much as I wish you would.
Only I can do this; no one else will do.

They little know they have written the truth
on the sign above my head
to them it's mockery, yet some know the truth
But where were they when I was tried and accused?
Peter has denied me, Judas is gone
Where are those who loved me, now my time has come

Why have you forsaken me?
I'm cold and afraid,
feel worse than the most evil of men -
more self righteous that a Pharisee
and crueller than the bloodthirsty tyrants yet to come
I feel weak, torn, deprived and alone
my soul cries desperately; don't leave me, find me a home.
I felt the burden of sin, with each nail driven in
and know I have cried for that which cannot be won
Darkness envelops the land and now I know:
into your hands my spirit goes, from my side the blood of life flows
and I know, after hours of agony,
I know that it is finished; my dying breath brings them life
It is so; for I was born to die.

   Melanie Dent

Hidden Treasure

I read poetry to my children,
All the time when they were young.
Not just nursery rhymes, but poems
That the old-time Minstrels sung.

Poetry is not elitist,
Who claim it is are very wrong.
It is a way of telling stories,
Without music, but in song.

Tennyson, Scott, and both Rossetti's,
Housman, Noyes and De La Mare,
All are poets telling stories,
Tales that children love to hear.

So I read poetry to my children,
However little they might be.
I pointed out the treasure chest,
And to each one gave the key.

Sheila S Thompson

Love Song

Time is ephemeral
Transience its essence.
Future present is, now past
But we are.

Being
We anticipate the future
We recollect the past
Being
We most neglect the present.

We cannot hold the moment
We cannot grasp it in our hands
But perhaps in time that's future
You'll hear with your inner ear
My voice read out these words dear
And know that I am near.

Hermione Evans

Motherhood

First two made one in marriage blessed by God
Then in due time a wondrous thing occurs
When consummation brings the fruit of love
And deep within one's being new life stirs.
Then microscopic cells will multiply, the tiny foetus grows until the
dawn

Of motherhood when on the natal day
Fulfilment comes at last - a child is born.
Now frequent cuddling and close caress
Will make the bonding that reduces fears
For it instils security and trust
That lead to confidence in later years.
In early days dependence is complete
Until beyond the home his world extends
New skills are learnt and social contacts made
And gradually for himself he fends.
As childhood days go by some discipline
Must go along with tender loving care
So when the young go out into the world
Their attitudes and judgements will be fair.
In teenage years some problems there will be
And these may well cause family stress and strain
But adolescence passes and in time the loving family ties prevail
again.

The years go by, the child's become a man
Or woman growing up in truth and grace
The strings are cut and rightly so, for then
The adult in society has a place.
It seems as if one's task has now been done
But motherhood's a never-ending state
And offspring who are loved and then released
Their years of care will now appreciate.

Marcelle Williams

Shell Song

A shell
Is not a bell
And yet it brings
The lingering lilt
Of ringing.
Bringing sea sounds
Of softly shifting sands
And pebbles tossed against the shore.
Ringing, ringing, in my ears
Filling my eyes with childhood tears.

A shell
Is not a bell
And yet it tolls
With hollow sounds
Of wind and waves
That echo far from distant caves.
Tolling, tolling, in my ears
Filling my desolate heart
With longing
To turn back the years.

Beryl L Lambert

Our Destiny

I told you to look around the world,
to tell me who you saw.
But all along I knew
I was the one you'd waited for.
I look into your eyes
and beneath your face, I see.
This love I hold for you,
you also have for me.
So why do you fight,
what is so right
you know I could never hurt you.
So believe me, when I say my love is true.
For with every beat of my heart, I'll just love you more
it feels like what, I've been put on this earth for
and so my love take my hand
and together we will travel this great land.
We'll walk across the mountains
We'll sail across the seas
together you and me.
Just the way it was meant to be.
For it was written long ago,
up above in the stars,
engraved upon our hearts,
that when we met,
we would never part.
So my darling, just let it be,
and stay with me.
Give in to destiny.

Sandra Heath

Life's Reflections

Taking a deep look inside my heart,
Wondering just where to start.
Casting my mind back, I will try,
Sincerely hoping you will not cry.
At the words written down here,
Some are sad, others bring cheer.
To do a good deed, makes one feel great,
What picture of beauty can we create.
If in life, even for a little while,
We can give someone a big bright smile.
Forget our problems, try to be kind,
Offer to lend a hand, to someone blind.
Although at times they do run wild,
Be ready to help that needy child.
As life goes on, we all grow old,
How many stories from them are told.
Before it is too late, and our life reaches its end,
Try to look on everyone as a friend.
Although a mixture of joy and strife,
Let satisfaction be your, Reflection of Life.

June F Allum

In A Bitter Time . . .

It is a bitter time
And an unhappy time
Perhaps, to send you flowers
- So brief, their perfumed hours.
Yet you may understand
If not - withdraw your hand
Quietly let them die
And without one sigh
Forget what lies behind
- The passion of the mind,
Withdrawn, austere, alone,
In this world not at home.
Words could not declare it
Petals, too, but tear it.

The Diners

Eating
treating
ourselves
with much zest.
Killing
filling
ourselves
with the best.
            Hungering
            mongering
            themselves
            for scraps
            of hard bread.
            Willing
            drilling the
            themselves
            to live half fed.

Can I relish the meat
you carve
when below in the street
they starve?
Aren't you aware
how damned unfair . . .

            Oh come
                come!
You're unnerved . . .

Dinner is served.

J Drewell North

The Crocodile
(Based on Rudyard Kipling's 'The Elephant's Child')

Here I am,
I'm lying low,
I'm bathing in,
The Limpopo,
I'm sitting here,
Waiting for dinner,
I'm sly and mean,
And I'm a sinner!

My patience it will,
Be your Death,
For look at me,
And take a breath,
I'll guarantee,
It will be your last,
For my teeth are sharp,
And my brains are fast.

Something is,
Approaching me,
Please wait a bit.
It's time for tea,
Right now he's,
Stepping on my back,
Open up my jaws and . . .

Whack!

    Duncan Cook

The Unwelcome Visitor

Your silent face stares at me, unknowing.
The rails rumble beneath us, rhythmically.
Through the grimy, glass windows scenes of green pass by.
Your mind and mine have no connection.

Our train draws slowly into the station,
like a worm slithering along the track.
We halt, and wait.

My cancer halts.
It slithered into my body like the
silent worm emerging from the upturned soil.
An uninvited, unwelcome visitor.

You are gazing out of the window
and your world seems so distant from mine.
My damaged body is so imperfect compared to yours.
My clothes conceal an absence of which you guess nothing.

Oxford approaches and you prepare to leave,
unfolding your fleecy coat
and reaching up for your heavy bag of possessions.

I look into your tired eyes
and feel your burden,
and I begin to wonder

Maybe, just maybe, cancer has
visited you too?

 Jane Snell

Millennium 2000

We move into the Millennium
Leaving the past behind.
The sorrows, the fears,
The joy of those years
Now left behind
For others to find.
Within the history books events they will discover.
The good, the bad and the very sad.
All are there within the covers.
Next Volume 2000 shiny new.
Blank pages are on view.
How will they be filled?
Only time will tell
As they ring the Millennium bell.

Partricia M Farbrother

No Room At The Inn

'No room at the inn', what a sad cry,
Mary was tired, her time was nigh,
Into a stable where animals lay,
There made a bed among the hay.

To bring to earth a bright new dawn,
Amid this scene the Child was born,
Hush my baby, be not dismayed,
Be at rest, in the manger laid.

During the night to the shepherds came
A band of angels praising Jesu's name,
Go to the stable to adore the Lord,
Then gladly spread the news abroad.

Then came the wise men from afar,
Guided by a bright lit star,
Into the stable, the Child to behold,
With gifts, frankincense, myrrh and gold.

'No room in your heart', is that the cry,
Will you your Saviour still deny?
In my heart Lord, I want You to stay,
Forever with me unto endless day.

W C Niel

A Passing Day

The fatal fall of a star so bright
The final flicker of a flame so alight
The desperate desire of friends so dear
For the light that once shone to again appear.

Thrust into darkness we weep and mourn
For the diminished light from a seven born
Taken untimely to the eternal rest place
Thanks we now give for its loving embrace.

The flame is still felt though flickers no more
Touched by its warmth we shall ever adore
And cherish a gift held so precious and dear
One day from the week passed, yet with us so clear.

But why again are we put to this test?
To question our faith and the fate of us rest?
Others we know are in your safe keep
So please, dear Lord, take this Day now he sleep.

God bless this Day.

Robert G Picot

Soldier Laddie

Eh, soldier laddie
take off your boots,
the piper's now playing you a different tune.
Lay down your bayonet,
uncock the gun,
the sun is fading laddie,
the battle's been won.

Fight no more soldier laddie,
their calling you up to the light,
take off your tunic laddie,
spread your wings to fly.
Look back no more soldier laddie,
yes, she grieves for you back home,
she'll never forget her hero, laddie,
so let go of her hold.

The piper's playing the last post, soldier laddie,
laying to rest your comrades to arms,
twelve hundred red poppies for many soldier laddies,
in remembrance for the bravest of hearts.

   C Leith

Cinbad Lugen, To Ravicis' Eyes
(Part II)

In the frigid darkness of an ageless Winter
I saw a pair of bright blue eyes smiling at me.

I had never seen a pair of eyes
Quite like those that I witnessed,
Burning blue, bright as the Mediterranean,
On a Summer's day.

Her name was To Ravici,
And in her eyes I beheld her soul,
Wise yet innocent.
No, I have never seen a pair of eyes
Quite like hers.

Burning with the fire of intelligence,
Resting gently with the warmth of compassion;
Wearing the solemnity of wisdom,
Though bright with the purity of youthful innocence.
An enigma!

How to be wise yet innocent?
Only by a refraction of the Light of God, perhaps.

If I were not too shy I would gaze into her eyes
For a long, long time;
Lose myself, forget my pain.
And be warmed by a refraction of the Light of God.

Richard Elsey

White

Falling, dancing, whirling,
Silent beauty turning
Green white.

Small, light, floating, wind whipped,
Growing large, soft, ice tipped,
Soft white.

Falling thick, fast for hours,
Soft, menacing power,
Pure white.

Cascade, yet no hurry,
Whirling, beating flurry,
Deep white.

Fury stops. Changed weather.
Large flakes now lone feathers
Of white.

Clearing skies show iced trees.
Sudden snowfall leaves the
World white.

Katherine Dean

Life's Journey

Life begins so tenderly.
The road is long.
And time goes by.
Memories come and go.
Faces, places.
Family and friends.
The good things.
The sad things.
The mind is full.
One does not forget.
So we are thankful.
There are no regrets.

F S O Crawford

Wool Worth

The sweet sheep graze and roam,
Shed tufts of woolly wools,
Caught up on wood and wire,
Like spindles, spinners spools.

Now shearing time has come,
The sheep, accepting, still.
Their lost and lonely lambs,
Stand bleating on the hill.

With wool from sheep be shorn,
The shearer bundles fleece,
And eager spinners spoils,
Are woven cloth apiece.

God's gifts so freely given,
To each and every one,
Earth's riches all around,
The work by Him well done.

He gives us grace to be,
Tools for His work and praise.
Tempered in His fire,
And channels of His Peace.

E Acaster

Abbots Langley - Hertfordshire

My adopted village . . .
For twenty-three years now
My home.
From my privileged spot
Across from the park
I see the seasons
Change -
Marked by the noble oak
Losing its green mantle
And gaining it again.

The High Street shops
Have undergone
Radical adaptations -
Co-op into Wine Shop
And Video House,
The Sweet Shop, old fashioned
With its sugary jars
Now an Italian style cafe.
Restaurants abound as do
Take-aways, so the spicy smells
Of cooking fill the evening air, but
The chippy is still there . . .

Junior School grown much bigger,
And our Library now 'on line',
But the heart of Abbots Langley
Is still the 12th century church
Surrounded by it's Victorian cemetery
Linking us with the past -
Yet forging forward into
The New Millennium!

June Chase

Reminiscences Of The Millennium

The great Titanic sank on her maiden voyage,
John Logie Baird invented television,
Alexander Graham Bell gave us the telephone,
Sir Alexander Fleming, penicillin.

In Westminster Abbey, Elizabeth II was crowned,
Later, heir Charles was made Prince of Wales,
Princess Margaret married Lord Snowdon
And the Royal Yacht, Britannia, sailed.

The 1966 World Cup brought England glory,
Mandela from twenty-five years imprisonment was freed,
The first woman MP was Maggie Thatcher, a Tory,
Champion boxer was 'pretty' Mohammed Ali.

Heart transplants and test tube babies were created
Which thrilled many a sad heart to bits,
The one and only Elvis died at forty-two,
The Beatles had numerous No.1 hits.

Our men fought bravely throughout two World Wars,
President JFK's life was destroyed much too soon,
Edmund Hillary and Sherpa Tensing climbed Everest,
And men landed on the moon.

After all these events in the Millennium
We all wonder what will be the next big deal,
Perhaps men will land on Mars
Or dear little, goggle-eyed ET (Extra Terrestrial) will become real?

Florence Scott

AD1900 to AD2000 And Beyond?

The century began with a queen on the throne,
Of a mighty realm where no sun set,
Women, though, still ill-considered,
In a society with equality unknown;
Rich and powerful but with poverty too,
Quick to fight each distant threat.

The horrors of Armageddon scale derive,
In Flanders, as Europe's youth were culled.
No land for heroes with tormented minds,
Torn by nightmares and mentalities to rive;
Yet strangely from conflict change was born,
As memories of war were slowly dulled.

Still in poverty, the world in peril,
The poorest the first to be called,
To face once more danger and evil,
As nations succumbed to aggressive drill:
Survival was hard, the empire shrinking,
Images of Belsen, and all were appalled.

The mushroom cloud, a potential shroud,
A planet perilously poised apace,
On the brink of an eternal abyss,
As whispers of reason then became loud;
Reality of perspective finally faced,
When images of earth beamed in from space.

We're a beautiful speck in the cosmos vast,
This earth's a ball with a steady spin,
Unless we live in fraternal harmony,
The following century could be the last;
Vile hate brought misery and loss, but
When it dies, peace rides in, to win.

Iolo Lewis

Gratitude

To all GPs, Surgeons, Scientists - Nurses,
For their learning and their expertise,
Without health we can do nothing.

In suicidal agony - deep despair - bedridden,
Unable to plant and prune the garden that I love,
Unable to pedal and play the organ,
One man alone was my salvation -
The clever, caring, understanding surgeon
Who in just two hours of surgery,
Cut away the rotten bone, inserting a metal pin,
Freeing me from pain to prune and plant again.

Giving the love of life anew - to view the setting, rising sun
- the morning dew.
How can I ever thank him
For this heaven sent golden miracle?

Irene S Brown

Littondale Serenade
(For RJH)

Pen-y-ghent and Arncliffe Cote
Guard lovingly 'The Dale',
secretly winding westwards,
vistas of perfect scale.

Skirfare's stream and Litton's ford,
in winter's rush or summer's drought,
cascading over pavements,
peat-stained pools of brown trout.

Limestone walls and hay meadows,
grass newly cut in rows,
both stretching up to heaven,
as far as tractored man goes.

Meadowsweet and mimulus,
soft murmurings of bees,
clambering over clover,
fanned by halcyon breeze.

Frail harebell and scabious,
serene contrasts of blue;
clustering by the wayside,
geraniums' purplish hue.

Shrill curlew and sparrowhawk,
still encircling the fell,
swooping on hapless creatures
whose brief lives none can tell.

Long-standing ash and rowan tree,
yet maturing fruit and seed;
the only remnants in Wharfedale
not devoured by man's greed.

Littondale, once Amerdale,
deep slumbering and so still -
long vanished Foxup's farmers
and schoolhouse in Halton Gill.

Hot baguettes and Beaujolais
now replacing older ways.
Restored barns and starred hotels
have seen far prouder days

Joan I Hands

The Common Market

The Government said join have no fears
But things have changed over the years
Two hundred and forty pence to a pound
Now just a hundred we have lost ground
Pounds and ounces have faded away
Now we have kilos and again must pay
Lost pints and gallons a few years ago
Replaced by litres and to our pocket a blow
The market is no good to you or to me
For now we have lost the old duty free
Now the Euro they want us to take
But if we do it's another mistake
To us all these things are a blow
And nothing has changed for those in the know

R C Hill

When God Became A Man

To Soldier, Sailor, Captain, King,
To wealthy, powerful or strong;
To Caesar's dynasty or Ming,
He could have chosen to belong -
    When God became a Man.

In comfort, affluence and power
He could have chosen to be born.
Yet he chose to make his bower
In Bethlehem's stable, cold, forlorn -
    When God became a Man.

He could have chosen some great City;
Alexandria, Antioch or Rome,
Jerusalem or Jericho, yet He
Chose Nazareth to be His home -
    When God became a Man.

Creator of the Universe,
Lord of Lords, Almighty King!
Sought no wealth, nor power perverse,
But came to men the word to bring -
    Of God's love for Man.

So soldiers, sailors, captains, kings,
you rich and poor, weak and strong,
Chorus as the whole world rings
With shouts of joy and bursts of song -
    To God become a Man!

Paul M S Pinto

Severed Heart

They cut me down to make way for other feet
I could not advance or retreat
but stood my ground the only home I've known
where they have choice I have none
I shall not rot graciously away
making soft their path
but hang on tenaciously
and with a silent hollow laugh
cling to roots which grew before they crawled
find strength anew in limbs which they have mauled
take revenge for all the woodland lost
for they destroy and never count the cost
one day they will repent and have me set
in concrete shroud lest they forget
preserved one arboreal dinosaur
for them to stand and gaze at in awe
the remains of the last tree on earth.

Sonia Singer

Peace

Oh! For the sky of blue and white,
To bring on mental calm.
The wars that rage throughout the world,
Do civilisation harm.
The call to arms will not abate,
While tyrants are in power.
Governments must act before it is too late,
Or lose at the final hour.

The way to peace is through countries uniting,
To cast out all the evil minds.
Just put an end to the useless fighting,
Get rid of all the tyrant kinds.
Religious fanatics can help the Devil's work,
So beware of strict religious greed.
Peace will not come from bombs or dirk,
But only by satisfying people's need.

We know that peace is a fragile word,
In this world that we live in.
It is war and strife that is mostly heard,
Brought on by those mortal sins.
Let all people live a fruitful life,
Give peace a chance is all we ask.
So Government's stop wars and strife,
Think of the people get to that task.

W L Downes

Knowing The Worst

There were red flower petals
On the footpath -
Bright red small blossoms
Had fallen and strewn my way.
No birds, no squirrels -
Just blood.
My blood.
Until now the sad bad news
Had drained my body
Of everything - except those pretty
Disjointed pieces of jig-saw,
Randomly tossed from the spring shrub
With no effort of themselves.
The cold easterly had blown
And swayed the thin fragile branches,
Enough for them to leave their
Collective beauty
And drop their single colour
All under and around my dragging feet.

Janet Sellars

Redundant!

On Friday evening, my whole life changed,
I was made redundant!

I was frightened and shocked - what needed to be arranged?
I had been made redundant!

It was done in such a 'matter of fact' way,
'You are now redundant!'

Some people were upset - not knowing what to say,
You've been made redundant?

The powers that be, said there was nothing they could do,
You are now redundant!

A large contact was lost, it paid for you!
So you are now redundant!

Now I have to search for work, it is not easy,
As I am now redundant!

I am trying to think positive, even be 'breezy' -
Then suddenly I remember,
I am redundant!

I hope that things will work out soon,
As I'm redundant!

I'd even consider working on the Moon!
I hate being redundant!

  Derek J Day

Millennium Prayer

It's your world, my world, our world
as long as we stay friends
and live in peace together
until our journey ends.

It's your hope, my hope, our hope
that life will carry on
and keep that peace forever
when all of *us* have gone.

It's your love, my love, our love
that makes the world go round
and looks in ev'ry corner
until the lost are found.

It's your song, my song, our song
that makes the happy sound
which calls across each valley
and rolls along the ground.

It's your faith, my faith, our faith
that lights the path ahead
and links the generations -
the living with the dead.

Ellen Green Ashley

New Year Resolutions

From many friends all quite sincere
Comes the wish *A Happy New Year*
Said of course with a cheerful tone
For seeds of hope have now been sown
Printed on a card or better
Like older times in a letter
But before it can make its start
You really have to play your part
Now's the time for Resolutions
They do have some good solutions
Change is what living is about
So take the plunge or you'll miss out
Take your pick and remain in charge
The rewards indeed could be large
Start it steady but keep it up
That's how champions win the cup
You could become a millionaire
For fortune goes to them that dare
Well anyway the best of luck
All you need is an ounce of pluck

Harry Derx

Ups And Downs

Andrew used the upper bunk,
'Get *up*, get *up*' cried she,
so he got *up* and then got *down*
to heed his mother's plea.
At table soon 'Eat *up* your flakes
then get your breakfast *down*',
their house was high on Epsom Downs
yet dad went *up* to town!
At school sir told the class 'Line *up*
then enter and sit *down*,
now sit *up* while I call your names'
and put *down* Andrew Brown.
Next into worship they all went,
knelt *up* in silent prayer,
except that some knelt *down* instead
to show they didn't care!
So the day passed swiftly till
his homework caused him frowns
for he wrote *down* and then wrote *up*
Life's little *Ups* and *Downs*.

Owen Edwards

Youth

Fill me with your wisdom, charm me with your words,
relate to me of your last night, of your different kind of world.
Tell me of your hopes and dreams of yet to come,
and I will think of all the stupid things, I've already done.
'Relax' you say 'Take it easy' you must take time to play
while I try to see how much work I can fit into each day.
This life is so much easier than it used to be.
No more shutting out the draught before we have our tea,
our hands and face quite smutty through getting in the coal,
cold water in the tap, so we washed them in a bowl
with hot water from the kettle and a lump of Lifebuoy soap
that's what with families and children actually had to cope.
Well once again describe your new cloakroom and shower,
of your gold taps and gadgets and hidden power.
Yes! Tell me of your indoor heated swimming pool,
I know that's what's needed in every Village School
To stop street vandals, it's because they're bored.
There is money 'not claimed', why not use it from that hoard?
If each evening they had somewhere like that to enjoy
All the Dads in charge would say 'They are all good girls and boys'.
There is nothing like competition to bring out the best,
Make it fun, make it happy, let nature do the rest.
Soon we'll see the happy social evenings we enjoyed before TV
With a kindly discipline in some homes you do not see.
You laugh at people who take themselves too seriously,
You seem to live on rainbows as they chase across the sky.
I think you're right and I am wrong, I wonder why?
Your shoes are wide and sensible, you laugh an awful lot,
I think you're really lovely and I am just a clot!!

Millicent Colwell

Why?

Why are we humans, so thoughtless and vain?
Wanting all for ourselves, causing others such pain.
God made this world, with plenty to share.
So why are we greedy and cause such despair?

We have so much, while others survive
With little, or nothing so poor is their lives.
Yet we hug to ourselves, all the blessings God gives
No concern in our hearts, whether others will live.

So God touches hearts and there's folk who do care.
They do all that they can, to relieve the despair.
Take food and clothing to those who have need,
God uses such people, the hungry to feed.

J Tolhurst

Pesky Poetess
(To my daughter Heather)

Sitting in a car, like you do
Looking round idly, in the queue
I saw this lady driver grope
On the dashboard for an envelope
A pencil then came into sight
As on the paper she began to write
A few hurried words written there;
Her eyes closed, a silent prayer?
A flash of inspiration lit her face
Words flowed on at greater pace,
A toot from behind - 'Would you
Move forward just a space or two'
Lips moving she read off the page
(I hoped those behind forgot road rage)
Again a long and thoughtful look
More words flowing - like a book
As inspiration began to flow.
The traffic starts - what a blow
Little progress has been made ahead
The traffic lights are back at red.
Paper stretched over steering wheel
A few more words written with zeal
Then, at last, a look of delight
She reread it, obviously all was right
A brilliant smile relaxing to a smirk
Lights green, she sped off to work.

Gordon Jack Crisp

165

Green - God's Colour

As I look from out my window
Earth's fair beauty I can see
Which I know is God-created,
Every blossom, leaf and tree.
Such a wondrous world He's made us
What enjoyment we can know,
For it is the Father's pleasure
To have planted things that grow.
Our God fashioned birds and flowers,
Set the rainbow in the sky,
An amazing, vast creation
By this wondrous God on high.
As we gaze in awe around us
Colours, countless can be seen
But to me it's so apparent
That His favourite one is - *green.*

Winnie Goodson

Changing Scenes

Those of us born, in the early part of this century
Must surely look back in wonder, at the new things that have come to
be.
Radio, television, satellite, walking on the moon too.
Penicillin, joint replacements, all the transplants surgeons do.

Travelling to distant countries, so easy by aeroplane.
In our childhood was exciting, just to travel on a train.
Nearly every family possesses, at least one car or two.
How different to all the walking we always had to do.

National health, state pensions, benefit if poor.
No threat of the workhouse, for anyone any more.
People living so much longer, with all the discoveries that are made.
Of illnesses that once caused terror, we need not be afraid.

Now as the 2000th century is coming into view
We wonder, maybe with apprehension, what else man may do.
All the Internet shopping, will food in a pill we see?
Roads that are overflowing, what will the cure there be.

Will we see peace in those countries where there has been so much
strife?
All the terrible refugee situations, all that loss of life.
Man who has grown very clever, filled with lust and greed,
Always reaching out for more, things he doesn't need.

Let us give thanks for all the good things that have improved our lives
each day.
All the research for other cures, to ease us, on our way.

Now as we look forward wondering what will come
Let us give thanks for God our Father the never changing one.
Through all the changing scenes of life whatever they may be,
He always is there for us, our rock, our strength is He.

E Griffin

Traffik '99

Dear Mother Britannia
Who ruleth these Isles,
Across your broad bosom
Stretching for miles
Great layers of concrete now lie,
Creating great harm,
Giving cause for alarm.
Perhaps part of your Spirit may die!

Our diagnosis -
Arterial (Rd.) Sclerosis, in very large doses.
We're extremely sorry to say -
There's such a great build up,
Your land's getting filled up
With traffic that won't go away.

With your arteries blocked
And your air turning grey
Every one rushing round
In an unheeding way.
Crazy to get from point A to point B
On motorways - spoiling your lovely country -
Where will it end?
Wait and see -
For today we hear bridges about to collapse
Not surprisingly so
With the terrible weight of the massive trucks
That are passing to and fro!

Edna Davies

Forbidden Fruit
(Dedicated to my beloved fiancé Peter Bartholomew 1999)

Deep frozen in time
You, who taught me how to breathe!
Held the key and turned back time.
I found a meaning to it all for a while.
My spirit soars so high
And our hearts beat sweetly in symmetry.
Even while we dream
Apart, but only by the miles
I close my eyes and see
Your loving smile.
I feel so safe, so cherished and complete.
You gave me so much joy
I thought that I would die.
At least I know how
Wonderful the feeling of sweet love upon my soul.

A gift you gave me
To hold for evermore.
Hold on to my love
And know that I will never be untrue.
For there are people
Out there that will have
Our one heart
Beat as two.

Pippa Howard

Remembrance Sunday

As I was kneeling at the altar rail,
Waiting my turn between the Bread and Wine,
I saw a beetle, in a dead straight line,
March on collision course . . . it could not fail,

So fatally do time and motion meet,
To fall under the ponderous crab-like shuffle
(And though soft overshoes are worn to muffle
Footfall, soles are still hard) of priestly feet

Advancing inexorably as a tank.
I took the cup and closed my eyes and drank,
And when I rose the creature was no more

Than a smear on stone - and suddenly I saw
A million beetles marching, rank on rank,
And priest and people making for the door.

John Goudge

Tomorrow's Another New Day

I woke up early one morning
When the day had just begun
Lying in bed I looked through the window
And just caught sight of the sun.

I felt it was wrong to be lying in bed
On such a lovely, bright, sunny day
So I quickly arose, donned my old gardening clothes
And promptly downstairs made my way.

I decided to stay in the garden,
Working until mid-day
When the sun would be at its hottest
And too hot for me to stay.

My plan was good and worked very well
I was getting what I wanted to do done
There was just one task left that I needed to do
When a big black cloud came and blocked out the sun.

I went back indoors, not a moment too soon
For the cloud I had seen brought some rain.
There were loud claps of thunder and lightning as well
How long it would last there was no way to tell.

But there's always tomorrow and what it will bring
And whatever that is will be new
So let us not fritter our whole lives away
Wondering what tomorrow will bring us to do.

When tomorrow arrives - as it most surely will -
Let us do what needs doing with zest
And not worry or fret or get very upset
If we can honestly say
'Well, I did do my best'
And tomorrow's another new day.

Peggy C

Carnival

First the rumble in the street
From beating drums and dancing feet.
Then a crazy whirl of sound,
Cheers and music swirling round.
Nearer, nearer comes the crowd,
Laughing, singing, voices loud.
Clearer, clearer, hear the brass,
A single tune appears at last.

Majorettes, with marching feet
And twirling batons, match the beat
As lead by rows of brass and drums
The carnival procession comes.
Dancing, prancing comes the throng,
Joining in one joyous song.
Hearing cheering, others come
To join the revellers in their fun.

Hear the crowd all gasp and cry
As magic worlds on floats go by.
Fairy castles, foreign lands,
Pirate ships . . . the last big bands
Blaring, ending the display.
The crowd begins to drift away
Fading, fading rumble of sound.
Left, the debris on the ground.

Geraldine Foy

Winter

O can you hear the winter song
Now where the white gulls wheel and sweep
And wild the roe deer leap along?
O can you hear the cold earth sigh in sleep?

I can hear the whisper of the rain
Where the lake stream softly christens
The winter grass and trembles on again
To pools where sunlight faintly glistens.

I can see the waters gleam
Where the heron greets the dawn
And sunlight gilds the stream
By the feet of the thirsty fawn.

And I can find a new delight
Upon the winter plain
And in the silence of the night
I can find new peace again.

Uvedale Tristram

Seasonal

October cold chill of night or day.
Those wintered stored clothes now
being part of our wardrobe again.
What pleasure pre summer to store them away.
Media tells us we can expect frosty morning.
Plants also flowers then can cause to die.
But they have given us such beauty
to indulge in from months gone by.
Those darker mornings, darker nights.
Heating now put on remembering
how we have been able to leave it off
in our daylight hours of summer,
such delight.
Those thoughts when in a cosy situation
to move makes you wish you could linger more.
But our seasons change we adapt,
we love magic of character of each season
because each change leaves a memory of past to store.

Victoria Joan Theedam